VEGETARIAN FOOD

CHARMAINE SOLOMON

D1740953

HAMLYN

Published 1993 by Hamlyn Australia,
a part of Reed Books Australia,
22 Salmon Street, Port Melbourne, Victoria 3207
a division of Reed International Books Australia Pty Limited

Copyright © Charmaine Solomon 1993
Copyright © photographs Rodney Weidland 1993

All rights reserved. Without limiting the rights under copyright
above, no part of this publication may be reproduced, stored in or
introduced into a retrieval system, or transmitted in any form or
by any means (electronic, mechanical, photocopying, recording or
otherwise), without the prior written permission of both the
copyright owner and the publisher.

Photographs by Rodney Weidland
Styling by Margaret Alcock
Food cooked by Jill Pavey, Romany de Silva and Deborah Solomon.
China: Countryware by Waterford and Wedgwood Australia Limited.
Typeset in 9½ on 12pt Berkeley Old Style Book by Midland Typesetters
Produced in Hong Kong by Mandarin Offset

National Library of Australia
    cataloguing-in-publication data:

Solomon, Charmaine.
    Vegetarian food.

    Includes index.
    ISBN 0 947334 60 2.

    1. Vegetarian cookery. 2. Cookery, Oriental. I. Title. (Series:
    Asian cooking library).

641.5636

INTRODUCTION

I hope you get as much pleasure as I do from visiting growers' markets or even a local greengrocer. Fruit and vegetables are so good to look at—colourful and with a variety of shapes and sizes and flavours that never cease to fascinate. I purchase what looks freshest and most tempting . . . usually what is in season and therefore the best value.

So that you can do the same, and then easily find recipes for what you have purchased, this book is divided into vegetable types—seeds, pods and sprouts; fruits; leaves, stems and flowers; roots, tubers and bulbs; mixed vegetable dishes.

There is a chapter on the all-important vegetarian protein sources such as lentils, soy bean products and fresh cheeses; and a chapter on grains, as these are the staple foods with which vegetables are eaten.

The art of delicately spicing vegetables is a skill that has reached a peak of perfection in India, where most of the population are vegetarian by preference. While strict vegetarianiasm is not as widespread elsewhere, nevertheless exquisite vegetarian specialties are to be found.

Cook vegetables and eat them immediately—each time they are reheated, valuable vitamins are lost. The dishes presented here provide examples from all over Asia and feature vegetables as the focus of meals, rather than as mere accompaniments to other fleshy dishes. Offer them proudly, eat them with enjoyment.

SPICE BLENDS

Having these blends made up and stored will make it easy and quick to cook vegetarian meals.

One of the most important blends, using whole seeds instead of ground spices to flavour food delicately.

PANCH PHORA (WHOLE SEED MIX)
Makes about ½ cup

- 2 tablespoons brown or black mustard seeds
  - 2 tablespoons kalonji (nigella) seeds
    - 2 tablespoons cummin seeds
    - 1 tablespoon fenugreek seeds
    - 1 tablespoon fennel seeds

Combine in a screwtop jar and store out of sunlight. Before measuring required amount, shake jar to distribute seeds.

I urge every cook to make their own garam masala. There is just no comparison between commercial products and what you can produce when the main consideration is quality, not price. Keep in a screwtop jar in the freezer and it will retain its fragrance for a long time.

GARAM MASALA (FRAGRANT GROUND SPICES)
Makes about 1 cup

- ½ cup coriander seeds
- ¼ cup cummin seeds
- 2 tablespoons whole black peppercorns
- 3 teaspoons cardamom seeds
- 5 small cinnamon sticks, broken into pieces
- 2 teaspoons whole cloves
- 2 whole nutmegs

Since some spices cook more quickly than others, roast each spice separately in a heavy based pan over low heat until they smell fragrant. Turn onto a plate to cool, and then grind to a fine powder in mortar and pestle, electric blender or coffee mill. Grate nutmeg finely and add to mixture. Store airtight.

Wonderfully versatile, this fresh masala adds flavour to rice and vegetables either at the beginning or end of cooking. Store for a few weeks in the refrigerator.

GREEN MASALA PASTE
Makes about 2 cups

- 1 teaspoon fenugreek seeds
- 8 cloves garlic
- 2 tablespoons chopped fresh ginger
- 1 cup firmly packed fresh mint sprigs
- 1 small bunch fresh coriander
- ½ cup vinegar
- 3 teaspoons salt

- *2 teaspoons turmeric*
- *1 teaspoon ground cardamom*
- *½ teaspoon ground cloves*
- *½ cup vegetable oil*
- *½ cup oriental sesame oil*

Soak fenugreek seeds in ¼ cup water overnight. Combine with other ingredients except oil and blend on high speed until a smooth purée. Heat vegetable oil and when very hot add purée and stir until mixture boils, then turn off heat. Cool, stir in sesame oil and pour into a jar. Add more sesame oil if oil does not completely cover the mixture. Use a clean dry spoon to remove paste. Add to stir-fried vegetables, stir into rice or add to curries for an extra boost of fresh herb flavour.

So few ingredients and yet such compelling results. Use in stir-fries, curries, or as a marinade for bean curd cubes before grilling. Gives a Thai flavour.

PEPPER AND CORIANDER PASTE
Makes about 1 cup

- *1 large bunch fresh coriander with roots*
- *1 tablespoon whole black peppercorns*
- *1 tablespoon chopped garlic*
- *2 teaspoons salt*
- *4 tablespoons lemon juice*

Wash coriander thoroughly, scrubbing roots and separating stems to remove sand which clings. Chop sufficient coriander to give 2 cups, loosely packed. Roast peppercorns in a dry pan for a minute or two until fragrant.

Put all ingredients into electric blender and blend to a smooth purée, adding a little water if necessary. If paste is made using mortar and pestle do not add lemon juice until after the pounding has resulted in a smooth paste.

Stored in a clean, dry, tightly stoppered jar this will keep in the refrigerator for weeks and is a useful flavour base for many dishes.

THAI CURRY PASTE
Makes about 1 cup

- 8 large dried red chillies
- 1 large onion, roughly chopped
- 1 teaspoon black peppercorns
- 1 tablespoon ground coriander
- 2 teaspoons ground cummin
- ¼ cup chopped fresh coriander roots and stems
- 2 teaspoons salt
- 1 stem lemon grass, finely sliced or 4 strips lemon rind
- 1 tablespoon chopped galangal in brine
- 1 tablespoon chopped garlic
- 1 tablespoon paprika
- 1 teaspoon turmeric

Remove stems from chillies and for less heat shake out seeds. Break chillies into pieces and soak in just enough water to cover for 10 minutes. Place in an electric blender with other ingredients. Blend to a smooth paste, stopping frequently to push ingredients onto blades with a spatula and adding an extra spoonful or so of water to assist blending.

GREEN CURRY PASTE   Use fresh green chillies instead of dried red chillies, and add 2 cups chopped fresh coriander leaves.

Seeds, Pods and Sprouts

Many of our most popular everyday vegetables come into this category—tender garden peas, sugar snap peas, snow peas, green beans of various kinds, okra, crunchy bean sprouts. Please feel free to substitute one kind for another when they are at the height of their season, remembering only to adjust cooking times. Tender young vegetables will need short cooking, while if they are older and tougher allow a little extra time. The thing to watch with pods is that they do need strings removed—especially snow peas and sugar snap peas—until they start breeding stringless varieties as has happened with green beans. Hasten the day!

5

SPICY FRIED BEANS
Serves 4 to 6

- *500 g (1 lb) tender stringless beans*
- *2 tablespoons oil*
- *1 teaspoon Panch Phora (see p. 1)*
- *1 onion, finely chopped*
- *1 teaspoon finely chopped fresh ginger*
- *1 or 2 chillies, seeded and sliced*
- *1 cup tomato purée*
- *salt to taste*
- *½ teaspoon Garam Masala (see p. 2)*

Wash and drain beans, top and tail and cut into bite-size pieces. Heat oil in a wok or saucepan and fry Panch Phora until mustard seeds pop. Add onion, ginger and chillies, and cook over medium heat until soft. Add beans, stir and fry until they are coated with oil. Add tomato purée, salt and Garam Masala, cover and simmer until beans are tender.

STIR-FRIED BEAN SPROUTS
Serves 4

- *1 punnet bean sprouts*
- *2 tablespoons peanut oil*
- *1 small clove garlic, bruised*
- *3 slices fresh ginger*
- *4 spring onions, sliced*
- *1 tablespoon soy sauce*
- *½ teaspoon oriental sesame oil*

Wash and drain sprouts and pinch off straggly tails. Heat oil in a wok and fry garlic and ginger without browning, until fragrant. Discard and add spring onions and bean sprouts to the flavoured oil, tossing over high heat for 30 seconds. Add soy sauce and sesame oil, serve at once.

In Indonesia, snow peas are called kacang kapri and make a delightful sayur (cooked in spicy coconut milk).

SNOW PEAS IN COCONUT GRAVY
Serves 4

- *375 g (12 oz) snow peas*
- *1½ cups canned coconut milk*
- *1 teaspoon finely chopped garlic*
- *1 teaspoon finely shredded ginger*
- *1 onion, finely chopped*
- *½ teaspoon ground turmeric*
- *4 strips fresh or dried pandan leaf*
- *sprig of fresh curry leaves or 2 dried daun salam*
- *1 stem lemon grass or 2 strips lemon rind*
- *½ teaspoon dried shrimp paste, optional*

Wash peas and remove string on both edges. Put 1 cup of coconut milk into a saucepan with 2 cups water and all ingredients except peas. Bring to simmering point, stirring constantly. Simmer, uncovered, for 10 minutes before stirring in remaining coconut milk and snow peas. Cook until bright green and still slightly crisp. Add salt to taste and serve with rice.

Note This sayur or white curry as it is called in other Asian countries may be used with any kind of vegetable in season.

This Indonesian bean dish can be fiery and is intended to be eaten as a sambal—in small amounts.

GREEN BEAN SAMBAL
Serves 6

- *250 g (8 oz) green beans*
- *1 tablespoon peanut oil*
- *1 teaspoon crushed garlic*
- *1 teaspoon sambal ulek or crushed fresh chilli*
- *salt to taste*
- *1 finely sliced onion*

Top and tail beans, string and cut in thin slices diagonally. Heat oil and toss beans on high heat just until colour intensifies and they are coated with oil. Add garlic and fry for a minute or so longer, then add sambal and salt. Beans should be crisp and half raw. Serve as a side dish, with onion slices added just before serving.

SNAKE BEANS WITH SAVOURY TEMPEH
Serves 4

- *500 g (1 lb) snake beans (long beans)*
- *2 tablespoons peanut oil*
- *1 teaspoon finely chopped garlic*
- *1 teaspoon finely chopped fresh ginger*
- *125 g (4 oz) tempeh, finely chopped*
- *2 tablespoons soy sauce*

Wash and dry beans well, top and tail and cut into bite-size lengths. Heat 1 tablespoon oil in a wok and stir-fry beans on high heat for 2 minutes, scoop into a bowl and return wok to heat. Add remaining oil and on gentle heat fry garlic and ginger until fragrant and starting to turn golden. Add tempeh and stir-fry until golden. Add soy sauce, beans and ¼ cup water, cover and simmer. Serve with rice.

STIR-FRIED SUGAR SNAP PEAS, THAI STYLE
Serves 6

- 500 g (1 lb) sugar snap peas
- 1 bright red capsicum
- 2 tablespoons peanut oil
- 1 teaspoon finely chopped garlic
- 2 teaspoons sliced red chilli
- 2 tablespoons Maggi Seasoning (see Note)
- 2 teaspoons fish sauce or light soy sauce
- 1 teaspoon green peppercorns
- 2 teaspoons sugar
- ½ teaspoon cornflour

Wash and dry sugar snap peas and remove strings. Cut capsicum into strips about same length as peas.

Heat oil in a wok and on low heat stir-fry garlic and chilli for about 15 seconds. Add peas and toss over medium high heat for 1 to 2 minutes. Have Maggi Seasoning, fish or soy sauce, slightly crushed green peppercorns, sugar and cornflour mixed together and pour into wok. Stir and cook until sauce thickens. Cover and simmer on low heat for a minute or two.

Note   Maggi Seasoning is a readily available substitute for Golden Mountain Sauce.

This is an ideal salad to take on a picnic—no lettuce or other greens to go limp, and since it is served at room (or outdoor) temperature, there is no need for keeping it in a refrigerated container. What could be easier! The only warning I would give is not to add the spring onions until just before serving. Take the spring onions whole, slice them and add at the last minute. We are all familiar with how strong and unpleasant onions can smell if they are cut and left for any length of time!

BEAN SPROUT, NOODLE AND OMELETTE SALAD
Serves 4 to 6

- 250 g (8 oz) fresh bean sprouts
- 250 g (8 oz) egg noodles
- 4 spring onions
- 3 eggs
- ½ teaspoon salt
- big pinch of white pepper
- 1 tablespoon peanut oil
- 2 tablespoons oriental sesame oil
- 3 tablespoons light soy sauce
- ½ teaspoon sugar

Wash and drain bean sprouts and pinch off straggly tails. If noodles are in tight bundles, soak in a bowl of warm water while bringing a saucepan of lightly salted water to the boil. (This loosens the strands and they cook evenly.) Take noodles from soaking water, drop into boiling water and cook for 2 to 3 minutes, until tender. Drain in a colander and run cold water through to cool. Drain again. Slice 2 spring onions and set aside. Finely chop remainder. Beat eggs, season with salt and pepper and stir in chopped spring onions.

Heat a wok or frying pan and grease lightly with a little peanut oil and make thin, flat omelettes until egg is used up. Turn onto a plate and leave to cool, then roll up and cut into fine slices.

In a bowl combine noodles, bean sprouts and sliced spring onions. Combine sesame oil, soy sauce and sugar, pour over and toss well. Add strips of omelette and mix again. Serve cold or at room temperature.

A Chinese-style dish which makes a feature of beans and is delicious to eat on its own.

BEANS WITH GINGER
Serves 3 to 4

- *500 g (1 lb) green beans*
- *2 tablespoons peanut oil*
- *8 or 10 thin slices fresh ginger*
- *½ cup hot stock or water*
- *½ teaspoon sugar*
- *½ teaspoon salt*
- *½ teaspoon oriental sesame oil*

Wash beans and dry well. Top, tail, and if necessary string before cutting into bite-size lengths.

Heat a wok, add oil and when hot add beans and ginger and stir-fry for 3 to 4 minutes or until beans turn brighter green and are coated with oil. Pour in hot stock or water, add sugar and salt, cover and allow beans to steam for 4 to 5 minutes or until tender but still crisp. Sprinkle sesame oil over and toss well, serve at once.

Okra is not very well known in Western countries, but is one of the most popular vegetables in Asia and the Middle East. It originated in Africa and naturally enough was taken to the New World. It is widely used in Creole cookery. When buying okra, it is important to choose small, tender beans rather than large, well seasoned ones. The test of tender okra is to bend the thin tip—if fresh and tender it will snap clean off but if old and tough it will bend. Its main characteristic is a mucilaginous quality much prized as a thickener in gumbos and curries.

DRY-FRIED OKRA
Serves 6

- 750 g (1½ lb) small, tender okra
- 2 tablespoons oil
- 1 teaspoon black mustard seed
- 2 sprigs fresh curry leaves
- 1 onion, finely chopped
- 2 teaspoons finely chopped fresh ginger
- 2 teaspoons ground coriander
- 1 teaspoon ground cummin
- 1 teaspoon ground turmeric
- salt to taste
- 1 teaspoon Garam Masala (see p. 2)
- lemon juice to taste

Wash and dry okra and cut across into thick slices. Heat oil in a wok or frying pan and fry mustard seed and curry leaves until seeds pop. (Cover pan or seeds will jump all over the stove.) Add onion and ginger, stir and fry until soft and golden before adding ground spices and stirring over heat for a minute longer.

Add okra, toss and fry until coated with spices, then cover and cook for 3 to 4 minutes until okra is tender but still crisp. Sprinkle with salt, Garam Masala and lemon juice and serve with rice.

Green Peas in Coconut Milk
Serves 4

- *1 kg (2 lb) peas in the pod or 500 g (1 lb) frozen peas*
- *1 tablespoon ghee or butter*
- *½ teaspoon cummin seeds*
- *1 cup finely sliced spring onions*
- *3 cups finely shredded outer leaves of lettuce*
- *½ cup fresh mint or coriander leaves*
- *1 cup canned coconut milk*
- *1 teaspoon Garam Masala (see p. 2)*
- *salt and white pepper to taste*

Shell peas or thaw frozen peas at room temperature, in the packet. Heat ghee in a heavy saucepan and throw in cummin seeds to fry for 30 seconds. Add spring onions, stir, cover and leave for a couple of minutes before adding lettuce and mint. Cover and steam for 5 minutes, then stir in coconut milk, peas, Garam Masala, salt and pepper. Cover and cook until peas are tender. If fresh peas are mature and need long cooking you may have to add a little water towards end of cooking, but frozen peas won't need extra liquid. Serve with rice.

FRUITS
AND GOURDS

Eggplant, pumpkin, zucchini, tomatoes, capsicums, cucumber, ridged gourd and bitter melon are only some of the 'fruit vegetables' which are so plentiful, colourful and downright delicious. Eggplant, particularly, is one of the most flavoursome of vegetables and is a mainstay of Asian vegetarian cookery. On page 20 is a recipe I created using Thai flavours and it has quickly become a favourite with everyone who has tasted it. Fruits like tomatoes and cucumbers, which may be used raw or cooked, give such different results but are delicious either way.

The larger the chilli, the milder and sweeter it is, so when you choose banana chillies or Hungarian sweet peppers, they aren't going to burn your socks off!

Banana Chillies, Stuffed and Braised
Serves 6

- 12 banana chillies or Hungarian sweet peppers
- 750 g (1½ lb) potatoes
- 3 tablespoons ghee
- 3 tablespoons oil
- 2 cups finely chopped onion
- 2 tablespoons chopped fresh dill or mint
- 1½ teaspoons salt or to taste
- freshly ground black pepper to taste
- 4–6 fresh hot chillies, seeded and chopped
- 2 teaspoons finely grated fresh ginger
- 1 teaspoon turmeric
- 1½ teaspoons cumin seeds, roasted and crushed
- 3 large ripe tomatoes, peeled, seeded and chopped or 2 cups canned tomatoes
- 1 teaspoon Garam Masala (see p. 2)
- 3 tablespoons chopped fresh coriander

Wash and dry chillies, slit one side from just below stem end and remove seeds and membranes. Prepare filling by boiling potatoes until tender, peeling and mashing.

Heat half the ghee and oil in a heavy saucepan and cook onions over medium low heat, stirring frequently, until soft and turning golden. Remove half the onions to a bowl and mix in dill or mint, salt, pepper and half the hot chillies. Combine thoroughly with potatoes, tasting and adjusting seasonings so mixture is well flavoured. Stuff banana chillies with this mixture.

Heat remaining ghee and oil in a frying pan and fry chillies until they blister slightly. Reheat cooked onions in saucepan with ginger and remaining hot chillies, turmeric and cummin. Stir and fry for a few minutes until fragrant. Add tomatoes and Garam Masala, cover and simmer until tomatoes are pulpy. Season with salt to taste. Lay chillies in a single layer in sauce and simmer for 5 minutes. Sprinkle with coriander and serve with rice or chapatis.

A cooling accompaniment to curries, but with a bit of bite—depending on the heat of the chillies.

Cucumbers in Coconut Milk
Serves 6

- *3 seedless cucumbers*
- *1 teaspoon salt*
- *½ cup canned coconut milk*
- *1 purple onion, finely sliced*
- *1 tablespoon lime or lemon juice*
- *1 fresh chilli, seeded and sliced*

Cut cucumbers into thin slices, sprinkle with salt and leave 15 to 20 minutes to draw out excess liquid. Rinse and drain. Combine with rest of ingredients and serve at room temperature since chilling makes coconut milk coagulate.

Sometimes it is possible to find the tender, sweet gourds which make mild and delicious coconut curries. When they are scarce, use cucumbers.

CUCUMBER OR RIDGED GOURD CURRY
Serves 4

- *1 or 2 ridged gourds (about 250 g (8 oz))
  or 4 seedless cucumbers*
- *2 tablespoons oil*
- *1 onion, finely sliced*
- *2 sprigs fresh curry leaves*
- *3 fresh green chillies*
- *2 cloves garlic, sliced*
- *6 slices fresh ginger*
- *1 small stick cinnamon*
- *1 stem lemon grass, bruised
  or 3 strips lemon rind*
- *1 teaspoon turmeric*
- *1½ cups canned coconut milk*
- *1 teaspoon salt or to taste*

Wash gourds and with a vegetable peeler remove sharp ridges. Cut into slices, about 2.5 cm (1 inch).

Heat oil in a saucepan and gently fry onion, curry leaves, whole chillies, garlic, ginger and cinnamon until onion is soft. Add lemon grass or rind, turmeric and coconut milk. If coconut milk is thick, mix with an equal quantity of water and if thin and watery use only half as much water or none at all, but total liquid to 3 cups. Simmer, uncovered, about 10 minutes then add gourd and continue to cook uncovered until vegetable is tender but still holding its shape. Serve with rice.

Note Snake gourd—deep green and a metre or more in length—is also cooked in the same way. Peel thinly or scrape skin (as for carrots), cut in thick slices and scoop out seeds, then proceed as above.

An acquired taste, perhaps, but there's something compelling about this bitter tasting gourd and it's said to be very healthy eating.

Bitter Gourd Sambol
Serves 4

- *250 g (8 oz) bitter gourds (also called bitter melon)*
- *1 teaspoon turmeric*
- *1 teaspoon salt*
- *½ cup peanut oil*
- *2 small onions, thinly sliced*
- *1 or 2 hot chillies, seeded and sliced*
- *2 tablespoons lime or lemon juice*

Wash and dry bitter gourds and cut into thin slices, about 1 cm (½ inch). Lay them in a single layer on a tray, sprinkle with turmeric and salt and rub into slices. Turn slices over and repeat on other side.

Heat oil and deep-fry slices until deep golden brown. This changes flavour from raw and very bitter to still slightly bitter but pleasantly so. Drain fried bitter gourd on paper towels. When cool and crisp scatter with onion, chillies and lime juice. Serve while bitter gourd is still crisp.

This vegetarian dish rivals fish, flesh or fowl in tastiness.

CHINESE-STYLE EGGPLANT
Serves 4

- *750 g (1½ lb) eggplant*
- *peanut oil for deep-frying*
- *2 teaspoons finely chopped fresh ginger*
- *2 teaspoons crushed garlic*
- *¼ cup dry sherry*
- *¼ cup soy sauce*
- *1 tablespoon vinegar*
- *2 tablespoons sugar*
- *2 teaspoons oriental sesame oil*
- *1 teaspoon chilli bean sauce*

Wash and dry eggplants and slice thickly.

Heat oil and fry eggplant in batches until golden brown. Drain on paper towels. Pour oil into a metal bowl and return a tablespoon of oil to wok. On gentle heat fry ginger and garlic, stirring until golden. Add remaining ingredients and stir until sugar dissolves. Return eggplant and cook uncovered, turning eggplant until sauce is syrupy and almost absorbed. Serve with steamed rice.

Note   If cooking in an iron wok, transfer to a dish immediately it is ready, or the acid in the dish can cause a metallic taste.

Versatile Pepper and Coriander Paste gives flavour to this tempting Thai curry.

FRIED EGGPLANT CURRY
Serves 4

- *500 g (1 lb) eggplant*
- *peanut oil for deep-frying*
- *2 tablespoons Pepper and Coriander Paste (see p. 3)*
- *1 cup canned coconut milk*
- *1–2 tablespoons fish sauce or light soy sauce*
- *5 fresh, frozen or dried kaffir lime leaves*
- *2 teaspoons palm sugar or brown sugar*
- *½ cup small basil leaves*

Cut eggplant into slices crossways, about 1 cm (½ inch) thick. If eggplant is very large, halve each slice. Heat peanut oil in a wok or frying pan and when hot drop in enough sliced eggplant not to crowd pan. Fry on high heat until deep golden brown on both sides. Lift out on slotted spoon and drain on paper towels. Repeat with remaining slices, then pour off oil from pan, leaving only a tablespoon.

Fry Pepper and Coriander Paste over medium low heat, stirring constantly, until cooked and fragrant but still retaining its green colour. Add coconut milk and 1 cup water, fish or soy sauce, lime leaves and sugar. Stir until mixture comes to the boil, then add eggplant slices and simmer, uncovered, for 10 minutes. Add basil leaves and serve with rice.

Note A variation of this recipe is to add an equal amount of potato slices. Fry separately until golden and simmer in sauce with eggplant. Increase coconut milk and water by half as much again.

CREAMY EGGPLANT RELISH
Serves 4

- *500 g (1 lb) eggplant*
- *½ teaspoon salt*
- *1 teaspoon ground turmeric*
- *½ cup raw peanuts*
- *1 small red capsicum, diced*
- *peanut oil for deep frying*
- *½ cup thick sour cream*
- *1 cup thick natural yoghurt*
- *1 clove garlic*
- *½ teaspoon sea salt*
- *1 teaspoon finely grated fresh ginger*
- *2 fresh chillies, optional*

Wash and dry eggplant, cut into wedges and rub over with salt and half the turmeric. Leave 20 minutes, blot on paper towels.

Heat ¼ cup oil and fry peanuts until golden. Drain. Stir-fry diced capsicum and remove. Pour in oil for deep frying and fry eggplant on high heat until golden brown outside and soft inside. Drain on paper towels. Combine sour cream, yoghurt, garlic crushed to a smooth purée with salt, remaining turmeric and fresh ginger. Spoon sauce on serving plate, arrange capsicum in centre and eggplant around. Garnish with peanuts and slices of chilli.

Serve this thick tomato purée on chapatis or buttered toast.

SPICY TOMATO PURÉE
Serves 4

- 4 or 5 large, ripe tomatoes
- 2 tablespoons ghee or oil
- 1 cup finely chopped onion
- 2 teaspoons finely chopped garlic
- 2 teaspoons finely chopped ginger
- 1 tablespoon sugar
- ½ teaspoon chilli powder, optional
- 1 teaspoon Garam Masala (see p. 2)
- salt to taste

Grill whole tomatoes over a flame or under a griller until skins split. Peel, seed and chop. Heat ghee and cook onion slowly until translucent and starting to colour. Add garlic and ginger, raise heat a little and stir until fragrant. Add tomatoes, sugar, chilli powder and Garam Masala, cover and cook until tomatoes are reduced to a pulp of pouring or spreading consistency, depending on use. Add salt to taste. Remove to a pottery or glass bowl.

TOMATO SALAD
Serves 4

- 2 large, firm red tomatoes
- ½ cup finely sliced spring onions or purple salad onions
- ½ cup chopped fresh mint or coriander leaves
- salt to taste
- lime or lemon juice to taste

With a sharp serrated knife dice tomatoes and combine with the onions and herbs. Season to taste, giving it a definite piquant flavour with lime or lemon juice. Serve as an accompaniment to rice and curries.

Make a coconut milk base as in Ridged Gourd Curry (see p. 17) and then simmer zucchini and cashews in it for a sensational vegetable to serve with rice.

ZUCCHINI AND CASHEWS IN MILK
Serves 6

- *750 g (1½ lb) dark green zucchinis*
- *1 cup raw (untoasted) cashew nuts*
- *1 onion, finely sliced*
- *2 sprigs fresh curry leaves*
- *2 fresh green chillies*
- *1 teaspoon finely chopped garlic*
- *1 teaspoon finely grated fresh ginger*
- *1 small stick cinnamon*
- *1 stem lemon grass, bruised or 2 strips lemon rind*
- *1 teaspoon turmeric*
- *1½ cups canned coconut milk*
- *1 teaspoon salt or to taste*

Wash zucchinis, top and tail and cut into thick slices. Soak cashews in hot water to cover for at least 30 minutes. Meanwhile, put remaining ingredients into a saucepan with 1 cup water and simmer uncovered for 20 minutes. Add cashews and cook for 10 minutes, then add zucchini and simmer for a further 10 minutes or until just tender. Serve with rice.

PUMPKIN IN COCONUT MILK
Serves 6

- *750 g (1½ lb) yellow pumpkin*
- *1 cup canned coconut milk*
- *2 onions, sliced finely*
- *3 cloves garlic, sliced*
- *5 cm (2 inch) stick cinnamon*
- *2 sprigs fresh curry leaves*
- *3 fresh chillies, split lengthways*
- *1 teaspoon turmeric*
- *1 teaspoon salt or to taste*

Peel and seed pumpkin and cut into cubes. In a large saucepan put coconut milk with an equal amount of water, add all ingredients except pumpkin and stir while bringing to the boil over medium heat. Reduce heat and simmer, uncovered, for 10 minutes before adding pumpkin. Cover and simmer until tender. Serve with rice and accompaniments.

TAMARIND CHUTNEY
Serves 6

- *2 tablespoons dried tamarind pulp*
- *½ teaspoon salt*
- *2 teaspoons brown sugar*
- *1 teaspoon ground cummin*
- *½ teaspoon ground fennel*
- *1 teaspoon finely grated fresh ginger*

In a small bowl pour ½ cup very hot water and immerse tamarind pulp. If necessary, add just a dash more water but not too much or the chutney will be thin. Leave to soak until cool, then knead and squeeze to disperse pulp and strain through a fine nylon sieve, discarding seeds and fibres. Stir in other ingredients, taste and correct seasoning.

When a vegetable has as much water content as zucchini or squash, it needs to be degorged before cooking if the flavour is not to be swamped by the amount of liquid it will exude. But the time spent doing this is well worth the final result.

Zucchini or Squash Dry-fry
Serves 4

- *500 g (1 lb) zucchini or squash*
- *salt*
- *2 tablespoons ghee or oil*
- *1 teaspoon cummin seed*
- *½ teaspoon kalonji (nigella) seeds*
- *1 onion, finely chopped*
- *1 or 2 fresh red chillies, seeded and sliced*
- *½ cup country style (thick) yoghurt*

Grate the zucchini coarsely into a large bowl. Sprinkle with 1 teaspoon salt, mix well and set aside for 30 minutes. Squeeze out all liquid with both hands. (This may be saved for a soup or vegetable gravy.)

Heat ghee in a wok or frying pan and fry cummin and kalonji until fragrant and cummin turns brown. Add onion and chillies and cook until onion is soft and golden. Mix in grated zucchini and stir over medium high heat until almost all liquid evaporates. Serve as is, or stir into yoghurt.

A cooling accompaniment to any curry meal.

CUCUMBERS WITH YOGHURT
Serves 6 to 8

- *1 large, thin-skinned cucumber or 4 small seedless cucumbers*
- *salt*
- *¼ cup finely chopped mint*
- *1½ cups thick sour cream*
- *1½ cups plain yoghurt*
- *lemon juice to taste*
- *3 teaspoons cummin seeds*
- *mint sprigs*

Wash cucumbers but do not peel unless you are only able to get the thick-skinned variety. Cut in halves lengthways and if seeds are well developed, scoop them out and discard. Cut cucumbers into small dice. Sprinkle with salt and place in a colander for 15 minutes to allow liquid to drain away. Rinse quickly with cold water. Leave to drain well.

Combine cucumbers in a bowl with mint, sour cream, yoghurt and lemon juice. Taste to see if more salt is required.

Toast cummin seeds in a dry pan for a few minutes, stirring constantly until fragrant and a darker brown. Crush seeds and sprinkle over yoghurt mixture. Serve chilled, garnished with mint sprigs.

LEAVES, STEMS AND FLOWERS

Leafy vegetables are the ones most of us had to be coerced into eating in our youth. If truth be told, some secretly resist them even in maturity; but when introduced to the same despised greens properly cooked, even the most reluctant develop a liking for spinach, cabbage, broccoli and others in this group.

When purchasing green vegetables, be especially watchful that they are fresh, crisp, firm and not yellowed or withered in any way. These vegetables are particularly good cooked in coconut milk with spices, as a white curry or sayur.

Asian market gardeners are providing us with an amazing choice of what is lumped together under the term 'Chinese cabbage' but try and get to know these vegetables by the names they are sold under and find out just how flavoursome are gai choy (mustard cabbage), gai larn (Chinese broccoli), Shanghai bok choy (miniature chard) and choy sum to name just a few.

An aristocrat among vegetables, slender stems of fresh green asparagus are a springtime treat.

ASPARAGUS IN SOY SAUCE
Serves 4

- 500 g (1 lb) tender asparagus
- 1 tablespoon peanut oil
- 2 tablespoons soy sauce
- 1 teaspoon sugar
- ½ teaspoon oriental sesame oil

Wash asparagus well, paying attention to tips and ensuring no fine sand lurks. Snap off ends of stalks—if fresh and tender they will snap easily and cleanly. If mature, cut a slice from the bottom and use a vegetable peeler on lower half of stalks.

Bring a large pan of water to the boil, add peanut oil and drop in asparagus. When water returns to the boil, cook for 2 minutes and then test a spear. If necessary allow a minute or so longer but remember asparagus should be crisp to bite. Lift out on a slotted spatula, drain on a clean tea towel and arrange in a neat bundle, all tips together. Cut into 7 cm (3 inch) lengths and arrange on serving plate. Pour over soy sauce, sugar and sesame oil mixed together and serve at once.

STIR-FRIED GARLIC CHIVE FLOWERS
Serves 2

- 1 bunch garlic chive flowers
- 1 tablespoon peanut oil
- 1 teaspoon oyster flavoured sauce or soy sauce
- 1 teaspoon cornflour
- ½ teaspoon sugar

Cut chive flowers in short lengths. Stir-fry in hot oil for 1 minute. Add remaining ingredients mixed with 2 tablespoons water and stir until sauce boils and thickens. Serve with rice.

THAI-STYLE ASPARAGUS
Serves 4

- 500 g (1 lb) tender green asparagus
- 2 teaspoons finely chopped garlic
- 1 teaspoon green peppercorns
- 1 or 2 hot red chillies, sliced diagonally
- 2 tablespoons Maggi Seasoning
- 1 tablespoon light soy sauce or fish sauce
- 2 teaspoons palm sugar or brown sugar
- 1 teaspoon cornflour
- 2 tablespoons peanut oil

Snap off any tough ends of asparagus stalks. Peel lower half of stalks unless very slender and young. Cut into 7 or 8 cm (about 3 inch) lengths. Mix garlic, peppercorns (crush them slightly with a fork) and chillies together. Combine Maggi Seasoning, soy or fish sauce (fish sauce would be used in Thailand), sugar and 2 tablespoons water, stirring to dissolve sugar. Mix in cornflour.

Heat oil in a wok and stir-fry asparagus on high heat until it becomes even greener. Add garlic mixture and stir-fry for 1 minute, then pour in liquid mixture and stir constantly until it boils and becomes clear and slightly thick. Serve at once.

Chinese cabbage, wongah bok, celery cabbage, Peking cabbage or Tientsin cabbage, they're all the same pale green, tightly packed, delicately flavoured vegetable. Delicious raw in salads too.

STIR-FRIED CHINESE CABBAGE
Serves 4

- *Half a head wongah bak*
- *2 tablespoons peanut oil*
- *1 teaspoon finely grated fresh ginger*
- *½ teaspoon crushed garlic*
- *1 teaspoon sugar*
- *2 teaspoons light soy sauce*
- *½ teaspoon oriental sesame oil*

Wash cabbage and shake dry. Cut across into 5 cm (2 inch) lengths. Heat peanut oil in a wok, add ginger and garlic and stir-fry for 10 seconds, then add cabbage and stir-fry for 1 minute, until all pieces come in contact with oil and hot wok. Add sugar, soy sauce and sesame oil and toss a further 10 seconds, remove from heat and serve at once.

Note   Iceberg lettuce is also delicious done this way, but needs only about 30 seconds stir-frying and must be eaten at once, while it still has its delightful crunch.

VIETNAMESE CABBAGE SALAD
Serves 4

- *Half a head wongah bak*
- *½ cup lime juice*
- *2 tablespoons sugar*
- *salt to taste*
- *½ cup shredded fresh mint*

Shred cabbage finely, cover and chill. Just before serving dress with other ingredients mixed to dissolve sugar.

Bok choy is chard cabbage with white stems and dark green leaves.

BOK CHOY, BRAISED
Serves 6

- *500 g (1 lb) bok choy*
- *2 tablespoons peanut oil*
- *6 thin slices fresh ginger*
- *2 cloves garlic, finely chopped*
- *2 tablespoons light soy sauce*
- *1 teaspoon sugar*
- *1 teaspoon oriental sesame oil*

Wash bok choy well, separating leaves. Shake dry. Cut bok choy into bite-size lengths, discarding any tough leaves.

Heat a wok and add oil, swirling to coat cooking surface. Fry ginger slices for a few seconds, add garlic and fry gently until pale golden, then add bok choy and stir-fry vigorously for 1 minute. Pour in soy sauce mixed with sugar and 2 tablespoons water. Cover and steam for 2 minutes. Uncover and stir-fry once more over high heat until liquid has almost evaporated, then sprinkle sesame oil over and toss to mix. Serve at once.

Note Gai choy or mustard cabbage is also done the same way. It has thick, bright green stems and a tangy, mustard-like flavour.

Broccoli with Peanut Sauce
Serves 4 to 6

- *375 g (12 oz) broccoli*
- *2 tablespoons peanut oil*
- *1 tablespoon Pepper and Coriander Paste (see p. 3)*
- *½ cup canned coconut milk*
- *1 teaspoon palm sugar or brown sugar*
- *½ teaspoon salt*
- *4 kaffir lime leaves, optional*
- *2 tablespoons crunchy peanut butter*
- *20 basil leaves, preferably lemon basil*

Blanch broccoli for 2 minutes in a little lightly salted boiling water, lift out broccoli and save cooking liquid.

Heat peanut oil and fry Pepper and Coriander Paste on medium low heat, stirring constantly until fragrant. Add coconut milk mixed with ½ cup cooking liquid and stir as it comes to a simmer. Stir in sugar, salt, lime leaves and broccoli, simmer for 5 minutes. Add peanut butter and dissolve in sauce, pressing with the back of a spoon to disperse. Stir in basil leaves and serve with rice.

Cauliflower with Green Masala
Serves 6

- *500 g (1 lb) cauliflower*
- *2 tablespoons oil*
- *1 teaspoon black mustard seeds*
- *½ teaspoon kalonji (nigella) seeds*
- *½ teaspoon cummin seeds*
- *2 teaspoons Green Masala Paste (see p. 2)*
- *or 1 teaspoon each grated garlic and ginger*
- *1 teaspoon salt or to taste*

Break cauliflower into florets, then slice each floret thickly, leaving a piece of stem on each.

Heat oil in a wok or saucepan and fry mustard, kalonji and cummin seeds, stirring, until mustard seeds pop. Add Green Masala Paste and cook, stirring, for 1 minute. Add cauliflower, toss with spice mixture, then pour in ¼ cup water and immediately cover pan with lid and use steam to finish cooking cauliflower, about 5 minutes. Serve with rice or chapatis.

STEAMED AND SPICED SPINACH
Serves 4 to 6

- *500 g (1 lb) English spinach or silverbeet*
- *2 tablespoons oil or mixture of ghee and oil*
- *1 teaspoon black mustard seeds*
- *1 teaspoon cummin seeds*
- *1 teaspoon ground coriander*
- *½ teaspoon ground cummin*
- *½ teaspoon turmeric*
- *½ teaspoon Garam Masala (see p. 2)*
- *salt to taste*

Wash spinach thoroughly in several changes of cold water to ensure any sand has been removed. Pick leaves only. If using silverbeet, cut along thick white stems with a sharp knife. Put leaves into a stainless saucepan with water that clings to them and steam over medium low heat about 10 minutes or until tender. Drain well, pressing out excess liquid. Chop finely.

In a wok or frying pan heat oil. Add mustard and cummin seeds and cover at once or mustard seeds will pop and scatter all over the stove. Add ground spices and stir for 1 minute. Add spinach and stir thoroughly, cover and cook for 5 minutes. Season to taste and serve with rice or chapatis.

Note Stems of silverbeet (sometimes called 'poor man's asparagus') may be steamed or boiled and served with melted butter.

Don't discard the stems of this very healthy vegetable—they are just as delicious as the flower heads.

BROCCOLI WITH CHINESE FLAVOUR
Serves 4

- 500 g (1 lb) firm broccoli
- 2 tablespoons peanut oil
- 1 teaspoon finely grated fresh ginger
- 2 tablespoons light soy sauce
- ½ teaspoon sugar
- 1 teaspoon oriental sesame oil
- 1 teaspoon cornflour

Wash broccoli well and divide into florets. Keep thick stems separate and peel if required. Bring lightly salted water to the boil and drop in the stems. Return to boil, cover and cook for 1 minute. Add florets and cook for a further minute, then drain immediately, saving cooking liquid.

Heat oil in a wok and gently fry ginger, stirring, for 1 minute. Add broccoli and toss in oil, then add ½ cup of cooking liquid mixed with soy sauce, sugar and sesame oil. Cover and cook for a further minute or just until broccoli is tender. Stir in cornflour mixed smoothly with a tablespoon of water and remove from heat as soon as it boils and thickens.

Gai Choy Relish
Serves 6

- *500 g (1 lb) gai choy (mustard cabbage)*
  - *1 red capsicum*
  - *1 cup sugar*
- *¾ cup cider vinegar*
- *3 teaspoons salt*
- *8 slices fresh ginger*

Wash mustard cabbage and trim off leaves—only leaf ribs and stems are used for their crunch. Cut into bite-size pieces about 2.5 cm (1 inch) long. Discard seeds and centre membrane of capsicum and cut flesh into squares. Blanch cabbage and capsicum in boiling water for 1 minute only, drain and cool in a bowl of ice water. When quite cold, drain again.

Put sugar, vinegar, salt and 3 cups water into a non-aluminium saucepan and bring to the boil, stirring until sugar dissolves. Boil 5 minutes, pour into a bowl and leave to cool.

Pour boiling water into a wide-mouthed glass or pottery jar, pour out water, pack in cabbage, capsicum and ginger slices. Pour over vinegar mixture, cover and store at least 3 days in refrigerator before using. May be dipped in a little sesame oil or chilli oil when eating.

Spicy Steamed Cabbage
Serves 6

- Half a savoy cabbage or white cabbage
- 2 onions, finely chopped
- 3 fresh green chillies, chopped
- ½ teaspoon turmeric
- ¼ teaspoon ground black pepper
- salt to taste
- 1 cup freshly grated or desiccated coconut

Shred cabbage very finely, wash and drain. Put into a large saucepan with moisture that clings, adding all ingredients except coconut. Cover and steam over low heat until cabbage is tender, stirring occasionally. Add coconut and stir over heat so that any liquid is absorbed by coconut. Toss to mix, serve with rice or as a warm salad.

Spinach in Spicy Yoghurt
Serves 6

- 250 g (8 oz) spinach
- 2 teaspoons ghee or oil
- 2 teaspoons Panch Phora (see p. 1)
- ½ teaspoon chilli powder, optional
- ½ teaspoon salt or to taste
- 1½ cups natural yoghurt

Wash spinach thoroughly and use only the leaves. Steam over medium heat, covered, until tender. Drain well and chop finely. Heat ghee or oil and fry Panch Phora for 1 minute, stirring, until mustard seeds pop. Add chilli powder and salt, fry 10 seconds longer, then turn off heat and cool. Stir into yoghurt to distribute spices, pour over spinach and mix well. Serve at room temperature or chilled.

CABBAGE IN COCONUT MILK
Serves 6

- *Half a tightly packed cabbage*
- *2 tablespoons peanut oil*
- *1 cup finely chopped onion*
- *2 teaspoons finely chopped garlic*
- *2 sprigs fresh curry leaves or 20 dried curry leaves*
- *1 x 400 mL can coconut milk*
- *2 stems lemon grass or 4 strips lemon rind*
- *2 or 3 whole green chillies*
- *salt to taste*
- *lemon juice, optional*

Wash and shred cabbage. Heat oil in a large saucepan or wok and gently fry onion, garlic and curry leaves, stirring frequently until onions are translucent and golden, about 15 minutes. Add coconut milk diluted with 1 cup water, lemon grass or rind and whole chillies. Stir as it comes to simmering point. Add cabbage and leave to simmer 10 minutes or until cabbage is tender but still slightly crisp. Check seasoning and add a generous squeeze of lemon juice if preferred. Serve with rice.

STEAMED CAULIFLOWER
Serves 4 to 6

- 1 medium-size cauliflower
- 60 g (2 oz) butter or ghee
- 2 tablespoons flaked or chopped almonds
- 1 teaspoon cummin seeds
- 1 teaspoon black mustard seeds
- ½ teaspoon kalonji (nigella) seeds
- ½ teaspoon chilli powder, optional
- salt and pepper to taste

Wash cauliflower, trim off stem and make 4 crossways slits in base with sharp knife to allow steam to penetrate. Put 1½ cups water in a wok and place the cauliflower in it. Bring quickly to the boil, cover and steam for 10 minutes or until just tender enough to be pierced with a skewer. Lift onto serving dish.

Wash and dry wok and melt butter or ghee. Fry almonds and whole seeds until almonds are golden and seeds fragrant. Add chilli powder, salt and pepper just before removing from heat, pour over cauliflower and serve.

LEEKS WITH CHILLI
Serves 4 to 6

- *2 large leeks*
- *2 tablespoons oil*
- *2 fresh chillies, seeded and sliced*
- *½ teaspoon turmeric*
- *½ teaspoon chilli powder*
- *½ teaspoon salt or to taste*

Wash leeks thoroughly, slitting them lengthways and making sure there is no sand or grit lurking between leaves. Cut off any old or yellow leaves, but all green leaves are used in this recipe as well as white portions. With a sharp knife slice leeks very finely.

Heat oil in a large saucepan. Add leeks, stir over medium heat for 5 minutes, then add remaining ingredients and mix. Cover pan, turn heat low and cook for 25 minutes or until leeks are very tender and reduced in volume, stirring occasionally. Uncover and cook until no liquid remains. Serve as an accompaniment to rice and curry.

In Chinese territory you'd ask for Ong Choy, in Thailand this is Pak Boong, but almost everywhere it answers to the common name of kangkung (u as in 'put'). If unavailable substitute chicory or watercress.

WATER CONVOLVULUS IN SWEET GRAVY
Serves 4 to 6

- *500 g (1 lb) kangkung or substitute*
- *1 x 400 mL can coconut milk*
- *1 finely sliced onion*
- *2 teaspoons finely chopped garlic*
- *3 slices fresh ginger*
- *2 slices fresh or brined galangal*
- *½ teaspoon ground turmeric*
- *½ teaspoon salt or to taste*
- *2 or 3 fresh green chillies*
- *1 tablespoon palm sugar or brown sugar*

Wash greens well and discard any tough stems. In a saucepan put coconut milk and an equal amount of water with remaining ingredients. Bring to boil, stirring, then simmer for 15 minutes, uncovered. Add greens and simmer for a further 15 minutes. For more substance, add 2 small potatoes, peeled and diced when starting to cook. Serve with rice.

FRESH MINT CHUTNEY
Serves 4 to 6

- *1 bunch mint*
- *1 cup roughly chopped spring onions*
- *2 or 3 fresh green chillies*
- *1 teaspoon salt*
- *2 teaspoons sugar*
- *1 teaspoon Garam Masala (see p. 2)*
- *4 tablespoons lemon juice*

Wash mint, shake dry and pick off enough leaves to make a tightly packed cupful. Put everything into blender with onions at the bottom, add 2 tablespoons water, cover and blend at high speed until smooth, or pound in mortar and pestle, a little at a time. Add lemon juice after pounding to a smooth paste. Cover and chill until serving. Best made shortly before serving as it will lose its brilliant green colour after some hours.

Salad is not just lettuce, nor does it have to be raw. Try using finely shredded parsley, tender passionfruit leaves, radish leaves or piquantly sour sorrel leaves. If you are aware of which wild leaves are good to eat, these will provide many more choices.

Cooked Green Salad
Serves 4

- *2 cups firmly packed edible green leaves*
- *1 small onion, finely chopped*
- *1 or 2 sliced chillies, optional*
- *½ teaspoon turmeric*
- *¼ cup finely grated fresh coconut (or desiccated coconut)*
- *lime or lemon juice to taste*
- *salt to taste*

Wash and finely shred leaves and combine with all ingredients except coconut in a saucepan with well fitting lid. Add 2 tablespoons water, cover tightly and steam over low heat for 5 to 8 minutes. Uncover, stir in coconut and toss over low heat until coconut has absorbed liquid. Serve with rice.

The common English name for this leaf, which looks like miniature violet leaves, is swamp pennywort. The botanical name is Centella asiatica. It was formerly known as Hydrocotyle asiatia (for the smaller variety) or Hydrocotyle javanica (for the larger leaf variety). It is credited with magical health-giving properties ranging from purifying the blood to curing nervous conditions, and two fresh leaves a day are said to give temporary relief from the pain of arthritis. Bunches of leaves are now sold in Australian markets and the plant in nurseries, where it is labelled 'the arthritis herb'.

GOTU-KOLA SALAD
Serves 4

- 1 or 2 bunches gotu-kola
- 1 small onion, finely chopped
- good squeeze lime or lemon juice
- 1 sliced chilli, optional
- 1 cup fresh grated coconut or ½ cup desiccated coconut
- salt to taste

Wash gotu-kola well and discard stems. Shred leaves finely with a sharp knife, combine with other ingredients and serve immediately. The flavour is slightly sour, slightly bitter, and grows on you. Some prefer this to be lightly cooked, in which case bring a tablespoon of water and ½ teaspoon salt to the boil in a wok or pan, add all ingredients and toss over heat briefly, stopping before leaves lose their green colour.

Roots, Tubers and Bulbs

Potatoes, carrots, beetroot, turnip, yams, onions and garlic all belong to this group of underground vegetables which are a staple of many cultures. Try to imagine what the food of any country would be like without the wonderful flavours imparted by onions and garlic. Onions can be used raw in salads, crisp and fresh and full of bite, or they may have their fierceness diminished by soaking in salt and rinsing them. Or they can be cooked gently for a long time, bringing out different nuances of flavour and caramelising their sugar content to give a totally different result. Garlic may be used raw and crushed, in tiny amounts, to add a special zip to a salad or relish. Or it may be cooked for a long while until soft and sweet, with a personality totally different from its raw brashness—in fact, it is used as a vegetable when treated thus. And try to imagine a cuisine that does not use that great staple, potatoes. I firmly believe there are more ways to cook potatoes in India than there are in Ireland!

Boiled Potatoes with Spices
Serves 4 to 6

- 750 g (1½ lb) potatoes
- 1 tablespoon ghee or oil
- 2 onions, finely chopped
- 1 teaspoon black mustard seeds
- 1 teaspoon turmeric
- ½ teaspoon chilli powder
- 1 teaspoon salt or to taste

Peel and dice potatoes, cook in lightly salted boiling water for 10 minutes or until just tender. Drain in a colander.

Heat ghee or oil and fry mustard seeds until they pop. Add onions and fry over low heat, stirring frequently, until soft and golden brown. Add ground spices and salt and stir, then toss in potatoes and mix gently but thoroughly.

Potato Yoghurt Salad
Serves 4

- 500 g (1 lb) new potatoes
- 1 teaspoon ground cummin
- ½ teaspoon chilli powder
- 1 teaspoon salt or to taste
- lemon juice to taste
- 2 cups natural yoghurt
- 2 teaspoons cummin seeds
- 2 tablespoons chopped fresh coriander

Cook potatoes in water until tender, drain, peel and cut into slices or dice. Combine ground spices, salt and lemon juice with yoghurt, pour over potatoes and mix. Toast cummin seeds in a dry pan, shaking or stirring constantly until they darken and smell fragrant. Turn onto a plate to cool, then crush in a mortar and pestle or between the palms, and sprinkle over potatoes. Scatter chopped coriander over and serve cold.

SWEET-SOUR POTATOES
Serves 4 to 6

- *750 g (1½ lb) potatoes*
- *2 tablespoons ghee or oil*
- *1 teaspoon black mustard seeds*
- *2 fresh chillies, sliced*
- *2 teaspoons ground coriander*
- *1 teaspoon ground cummin*
- *½ teaspoon ground turmeric*
- *½ teaspoon chilli powder or to taste*
- *½ teaspoon salt or to taste*
- *1 tablespoon dried tamarind pulp*
- *2 teaspoons palm sugar or brown sugar*

Peel and dice potatoes. In a heavy saucepan heat ghee or oil and fry mustard seeds until they pop. Add chillies and ground spices and stir for 30 seconds or until fragrant. Add potatoes, sprinkle with salt and about ¼ cup water, cover pan tightly and cook on very low heat for 15 minutes. Meanwhile, soak tamarind pulp in ¼ cup hot water and squeeze to dissolve pulp. Strain out seeds and fibres. Dissolve sugar in tamarind liquid. Add to potatoes, stir gently, cover and cook for a further 10 minutes or until potatoes are tender.

I have a passion for this preparation and when you try it you will understand why. Delicious with rice or chapatis, or simply on its own.

DRY POTATO CURRY
Serves 4 to 6

- 750 g (1½ lb) potatoes
- 2 tablespoons ghee or oil
- 1½ teaspoons Panch Phora (see p. 1)
- 1 large onion, finely chopped
- 1 teaspoon turmeric
- 1 teaspoon ground cummin
- ½ teaspoon chilli powder, or to taste
- 1 teaspoon salt or to taste
- ¼ cup chopped fresh mint or coriander
- 1½ teaspoons Garam Masala (see p. 2)
- good squeeze lemon juice

Peel and dice potatoes. In a heavy based saucepan with well fitting lid heat ghee and add Panch Phora. When mustard seeds pop add onion and stir occasionally over low heat until soft, translucent and starting to turn golden. Add ground spices and stir for a few seconds, add potatoes, mix well and pour in ¼ cup water. Cover pan tightly, cook on very low heat for 20 minutes without lifting lid. Shake pan occasionally to keep potatoes from sticking. Scatter chopped herbs, Garam Masala and lemon juice over, and a tablespoon more water if necessary. Cover pan again and cook a further 10 minutes or until potatoes are soft and a slight crust has formed on base of pan. Serve with chapatis or rice. Collect the crust too as it has great flavour.

Note This makes a great filling for savoury pastries called singaras. Make chapati dough (see p. 79) and roll thinly. Cut saucer-size circles and cut each in halves. Put a teaspoon of filling on each half, dampen edges and seal. When all are made, deep fry in hot oil. Drain on paper towels and serve with a dip such as Mint Chutney (see p. 40).

Spicy Mashed Potatoes
Serves 4 to 6

- *500 g (1 lb) potatoes*
- *2 tablespoons melted butter*
- *¼ cup boiling milk*
- *¼ cup lemon juice*
- *½ teaspoon salt or to taste*
- *½ cup finely chopped fresh mint leaves*
- *¼ cup finely chopped spring onions*

Boil potatoes until tender, drain in a colander, peel and mash while still hot. Add melted butter and boiling milk and mix to a creamy, fluffy consistency. Add remaining ingredients and mix well. Pile in a bowl or pat into a flat cake and garnish with mint sprig.

Beetroot and Yoghurt Relish
Serves 4 to 6

- *2 cups diced cooked or canned beetroot*
- *2 cups thick natural yoghurt*
- *salt and pepper to taste*
- *½ teaspoon Garam Masala (see p. 2)*
- *lemon juice, optional*

Combine beetroot, yoghurt and seasonings. If using canned beetroot there is sufficient vinegar to make lemon juice unnecessary but if using fresh beetroot, add sufficient lemon juice to make it nicely piquant. Chill and serve as an accompaniment with rice and curries.

Onion Salad
Serves 4

- 2 mild salad onions
- salt
- 1 tablespoon dried tamarind pulp
- 1–2 tablespoons palm sugar or brown sugar
- 2 firm red tomatoes, seeded and diced
- 2 fresh green chillies, seeded and sliced
- chopped fresh mint or coriander leaves

Peel onions, halve lengthways, then slice very thinly crossways. Put into a bowl, sprinkle with salt, mix lightly and leave for at least 30 minutes. Rinse in cold water. Drain. Pour 1/3 cup very hot water over tamarind pulp and when cool enough to handle, squeeze to dissolve pulp to strain through a fine nylon sieve and discard seeds and fibres. Stir in sugar. Combine all ingredients and mix thoroughly. Chill and serve sprinkled with fresh herbs as an accompaniment to rice and curry meals.

Fried Onion Sambal
Serves 6 to 8

- 4 large onions
- ½ cup oil
- 8 large red dried chillies
- ¼ lemon juice
- 1 teaspoon salt or to taste
- 2 tablespoons sugar

Peel onions and cut into thick slices. Heat oil and slowly fry onion until soft and turning golden brown. Snip chillies into pieces with scissors, shake out seeds and discard stems. Add to onions, cover and cook gently for a further 20 minutes or until deep brown but not burnt. Stir in lemon juice, salt and sugar. Serve with rice and curries.

CARROT RELISH
Serves 4

- 500 g (1 lb) carrots
- 3 tablespoons oil
- 2 teaspoons crushed garlic
- 1 teaspoon turmeric
- 1 teaspoon ground cummin
- 2 teaspoons paprika
- ¼ teaspoon chilli powder, optional
- salt to taste
- 2 teaspoons sugar
- 2 tablespoons lemon juice

Peel carrots and cut into fine diagonal slices. A food processor does this in no time. Heat oil in a pan with a well fitting lid and cook garlic slowly until mellow. Add ground spices and stir for 1 minute, then add carrots and mix well. Add ¼ cup water, cover and steam for 10 minutes or until carrots are tender. Add salt, sugar and lemon juice, mix well and serve at room temperature.

Use yams and sweet potatoes in the same way you would use potatoes,
judging cooking time according to variety being used.

Yam Curry
Serves 4

- *500 g (1 lb) yam or sweet potato*
- *oil for deep-frying*
- *1 tablespoon ghee*
- *2 medium onions, chopped finely*
- *2 teaspoons finely chopped fresh ginger*
- *2 fresh red or green chillies, seeded and chopped*
- *1 teaspoon ground coriander*
- *1 teaspoon ground cummin*
- *½ teaspoon ground turmeric*
- *½ teaspoon Garam Masala (see p. 2)*
- *1 teaspoon salt or to taste*
- *3 tablespoons chopped fresh coriander*
- *lemon juice to taste*

Peel and slice or dice yam. Soak in lightly salted water for 30 minutes. Drain well and dry thoroughly on paper towels. Heat oil and add ghee to give it flavour. Deep-fry yam, not too much at one time, until golden brown. Lift on slotted spoon and drain on paper towels.

Pour off oil, leaving about 2 tablespoons. Fry onion, ginger and chillies over medium heat, stirring occasionally, until onion is soft and golden. Add ground spices and fry for another minute, stirring. Add yams, sprinkle with salt and fresh coriander and toss over low heat for 5 minutes. Add lemon juice to taste. Serve with rice or chapatis.

MIXED VEGETABLE DISHES

In this chapter you will find delectable dishes which don't fit into the other chapters dealing with specific types. Here are a variety of combinations—potatoes and peas; spinach and pumpkin; bamboo shoot, lotus root and water chestnuts; and, because we don't have a separate chapter on mushrooms and other fungus, I'm sneaking them in here too!

STIR-FRIED VEGETABLES AND BRAISED BEAN CURD
Serves 4

- *12 dried shiitake (Chinese) mushrooms*
- *3 tablespoons peanut oil*
- *3 tablespoons dark soy sauce*
- *1 tablespoon sugar*
- *2 teaspoons oriental sesame oil*
- *125 g (4 oz) sugar snap peas, string removed*
- *250 g (8 oz) green asparagus cut bite-size*
- *1 small can mini corn cobs, drained*
- *8 squares fried bean curd, halved diagonally*
- *15 g (½ oz) dried wood fungus, soaked 10 minutes*

Soak mushrooms in very hot water for 30–40 minutes. Save water, squeezing out excess from mushrooms. Cut off stems and fry mushroom caps in 2 tablespoons oil till underside is golden brown. Add 2 cups soaking water mixed with soy sauce, sugar and sesame oil. Cover and simmer 30 minutes, adding a little more water if necessary. Add corn cobs and bean curd, cover and simmer 5 minutes. Trim any gritty bits from wood fungus, cut in bite-size pieces, stir in and cook 3 minutes.

In another wok heat remaining tablespoon oil and fry garlic and ginger for a few seconds. Add peas and asparagus, stir-fry for 1 minute, add 2 tablespoons water, cover wok and steam for 2 minutes. Toss with braised mixture and serve at once, with rice.

These crisp, lightly battered and fried vegetable fritters are popular with everyone—even those who dislike vegetables will be asking for more!

Pakorhas

Serves 4 as appetiser

- ½ cup besan *(chick pea flour)*
- ¾ cup self-raising flour
- 2 tablespoons ground rice
- 1 teaspoon Garam Masala *(see p. 2)*
- ½ teaspoon ajowan seeds
- ½ teaspoon ground turmeric
- ¼ teaspoon chilli powder, optional
- ½ teaspoon salt
- fine slices of potato, onion, cauliflower, eggplant, washed and dried leaves of English spinach, sorrel
- peanut oil for deep-frying

Combine flours, spices and salt with 1 cup water and beat to a smooth batter of coating consistency.

Prepare vegetables. Small potatoes are better than large. Peel and slice them very thinly. Peel onion, keeping the root end on and cutting in thin slices lengthways so there is a bit of root on slices to hold layers together. Cauliflower should be sliced thinly with a piece of stem to hold florets together. Eggplant (again small, rather than large) is left unpeeled and sliced fairly thickly. If large, slices may be halved. Wash leaves and dry thoroughly on paper towels—if large, cut in 2 or 3 pieces. (If you have a grape vine, try some very small, tender vine leaves—they are delicious!)

Heat oil for deep-frying and dip a few pieces of vegetable at a time into batter, then drop into oil until golden brown and crisp. Lift out on slotted frying spoon and drain on paper towels. Serve with Tamarind or Fresh Mint Chutney.

Note Pakorhas are also made with finely diced vegetables, mixed into batter and fried in spoonfuls.

POTATOES AND SPINACH
Serves 4

- *500 g (1 lb) new potatoes*
- *1 bunch English spinach*
- *2 tablespoons oil*
- *1 teaspoon black mustard seeds*
- *1 teaspoon cummin seeds*
- *½ teaspoon ground turmeric*
- *1 teaspoon ground coriander*
- *1 teaspoon ground cummin*
- *2 fresh chillies, slit and seeded*
- *½ teaspoon salt or to taste*
- *½ teaspoon ground nutmeg*

Scrub potatoes and cut into dice. Wash spinach thoroughly in cold water, discard tough stems. Steam over low heat in a large saucepan until wilted.

Heat oil in a wok and fry mustard and cummin seeds until mustard seeds pop, covering wok to prevent them spattering. Add ground spices, chillies and potatoes. Stir-fry for a few minutes, then add salt and ½ cup water, cover and cook for 10 minutes. Stir in spinach and liquid that has collected in the saucepan, cover and cook until potatoes are tender. Sprinkle nutmeg over and stir. Serve with rice or chapatis.

Eggplant Purée with Chick Peas
Serves 6

- *1 cup dried chick peas*
- *4 cardamom pods*
- *2 large eggplants*
- *2 tablespoons oil or ghee*
- *2 large onions, finely chopped*
- *2 teaspoons finely chopped ginger*
- *2 teaspoons ground coriander*
- *2 teaspoons ground cummin*
- *½ teaspoon turmeric*
- *1 cup chopped tomatoes*

Soak chick peas in water to cover for at least 6 hours. In a heavy saucepan put chick peas with fresh water to cover by at least 2.5 cm (1 inch) and cardamom pods, bruised. Bring to a simmer and cook, covered, for 1 hour or until tender but still holding their shape.

Grill eggplants over a barbecue or under a preheated griller until skins are blackened. Cool, peel and discard skin. Chop flesh roughly.

In a heavy saucepan heat oil and cook onions and ginger over gentle heat, stirring occasionally, for 20 minutes or until onions are soft and translucent, and turn golden. Add ground spices and fry, stirring, for 1 minute then add eggplant, salt and tomatoes, stir well, cover and cook for 30 minutes. Stir in drained chick peas and simmer, covered, a further 15 to 20 minutes. Taste and add salt if necessary. Serve with rice or chapatis.

SPICY DICED VEGETABLES
Serves 4 to 6

- 2 tablespoons ghee or oil
- 2 teaspoons black mustard seeds
- 2 onions, finely chopped
- 1 teaspoon finely chopped garlic
- 1 teaspoon finely chopped fresh ginger
- 1 teaspoon ground coriander
- 1 teaspoon ground cummin
- 1 teaspoon salt or to taste
- 2 cups diced carrots
- 2 cups diced potatoes
- 1 cup green beans, cut in short lengths
- 2 large ripe tomatoes, diced
- ½ teaspoon Garam Masala (see p. 2)

Heat oil in a saucepan and fry mustard seeds until they pop. Add onions, garlic and ginger and fry, stirring, until golden. Add coriander and cummin and fry for a few seconds, then add salt and vegetables and toss until coated with spices and oil. Add ¼ cup water, cover and cook on gentle heat for 15 minutes or until tender, stirring gently at 5 minute intervals and adding a little extra water if necessary. Sprinkle with Garam Masala at end of cooking. Serve with rice or chapatis.

STIR-FRIED VEGETABLES AND EGGS
Serves 4

- *8 dried shiitake (Chinese) mushrooms*
- *1 bunch asparagus*
- *1 red capsicum*
- *4 eggs*
- *salt and pepper to taste*
- *2 tablespoons peanut oil*
- *1 small clove garlic, crushed*
- *2 tablespoons soy sauce*
- *½ teaspoon sugar*
- *½ teaspoon oriental sesame oil*

Soak mushrooms in very hot water for 30 minutes. Squeeze out excess water, discard stems and cut caps into halves or quarters. Trim ends off asparagus and cut spears into bite-size lengths. Discard seeds and membrane of capsicum and cut into strips, then into bite-size lengths. Beat eggs slightly, season with salt and pepper.

Heat 1 tablespoon oil in a wok and fry eggs, stirring, until set. Remove from wok and add remaining oil. Stir-fry mushrooms, asparagus and capsicum on high heat until colours brighten, about 2 minutes. Add garlic, soy sauce, sugar and sesame oil mixed with 2 tablespoons water. Cover and steam for 2 minutes or until vegetables are tender but still crisp. Return egg and toss with vegetables. Serve with rice.

INDIAN-STYLE POTATOES AND PEAS
Serves 4 to 6

- *2 tablespoons ghee or oil*
- *2 medium onions, chopped finely*
- *2 teaspoons finely chopped fresh ginger*
- *1 teaspoon black mustard seeds*
- *½ teaspoon kalonji (nigella) seeds*
- *½ teaspoon turmeric*
- *1 teaspoon salt or to taste*
- *750 g (1½ lb) potatoes, peeled and diced*
- *375 g (12 oz) frozen peas or fresh peas, shelled*
- *½ teaspoon Garam Masala (see p. 2)*

Heat ghee or oil in a heavy saucepan and fry onions, ginger and whole seeds, stirring frequently, until onions are soft and start to brown. Add turmeric and fry for a few seconds, then add salt, potatoes and peas. Toss vegetables in spice mixture for 1 to 2 minutes, then pour in 1 cup boiling water, cover pan tightly and cook on low heat for 30 minutes. Add Garam Masala 5 minutes before end of cooking. Adjust seasoning and serve warm with rice or chapatis.

A famous Chinese vegetarian dish, many versions of which lay claim to the name, Lo Han Chai. *I have eaten it several times, including a deluxe version in a Buddhist monastery high on a mountain on one of the outlying islands of Hong Kong, in a superb, totally vegetarian meal, with rare ingredients. This version is pleasing and entirely attainable.*

Braised Vegetable Combination
Serves 4 to 6

- 125 g (4 oz) dried bean curd sticks
- 16–18 dried shiitake (Chinese) mushrooms
- 30 dried lily buds (golden needles)
- 15 g (½ oz) dried wood fungus
- 2 canned winter bamboo shoots
- 1 canned lotus root
- 1 small can water chestnuts
- 500 g (1 lb) fresh asparagus
- 1 can baby corn
- 3 tablespoons peanut oil
- 3 tablespoons light soy sauce
- 2 tablespoons hoi sin sauce
- 1 whole star anise
- 2 teaspoons cornflour
- 2 teaspoons oriental sesame oil
- 2 teaspoons sugar

There's a lot of soaking of dried ingredients, so line up some bowls. Snap bean curd sticks into bite-size pieces and soak in cold water for 20 minutes. Drain, return to bowl and pour boiling water over. Leave to cool. Soak dried mushrooms in very hot water to cover for at least 30 minutes. (If they are thick, high quality shiitake, it will take about an hour for them to soak through, but they are worth the wait.) Drain, squeeze out excess moisture (save soaking liquid) and trim off stems.

Soak lily buds in warm water for 30 minutes, drain, pinch off stem ends if tough and tie a knot in each or cut in halves. Soak wood fungus in cold water for 20 minutes, drain and cut bite-size, trimming off any gritty bits.

Slice bamboo shoots, lotus root and water chestnuts. Trim ends off asparagus, peel lower stem and cut in short lengths. Blanch asparagus for 2 minutes in boiling water, then drop into ice water to set colour. Drain baby corn.

Heat wok, add peanut oil and when very hot fry well drained bean curd, mushrooms and lily buds for 3 to 4 minutes. Add soy and hoi sin sauces and 2 cups mushroom soaking liquid. Add star anise, bring to the boil, then cover and simmer gently for 20 minutes. Add bamboo shoot, lotus root, water chestnuts and simmer for 10 minutes. Stir cornflour mixed with a tablespoon of cold water into the liquid until it boils and thickens. Lastly add asparagus, baby corn, wood fungus, sugar and sesame oil and mix well. Serve with rice.

Note Lily buds are available fresh in season and make a bright, attractive addition to this dish. These are the buds of a variety of orange and yellow day lilies, (*Hemerocallis* spp.) If using them fresh they do not need soaking and the stem ends don't have to be trimmed, being crisply tender. Look for them in Asian areas around autumn.

Spicy Spinach with Pumpkin and Nuts
Serves 6

- *2 bunches English spinach*
- *2 tablespoons oil*
- *1 teaspoon Panch Phora (see p. 1)*
- *2 onions, chopped finely*
- *2 teaspoons finely chopped fresh ginger*
- *½ teaspoon ground turmeric*
- *500 g (1 lb) pumpkin, peeled and diced*
- *1 cup raw cashews*
- *1 teaspoon salt*
- *½ teaspoon Garam Masala (see p. 2)*

Wash spinach thoroughly, trim off stalks and put leaves in a saucepan with moisture that clings. Cover and steam for 10 minutes or until tender. Drain, chop roughly.

Heat oil and fry Panch Phora until mustard seeds pop. Add onion and ginger and fry, stirring, until onion is soft. Add turmeric and fry a further few seconds.

Add 1 cup hot water, pumpkin, cashews and salt, simmer for 15 minutes adding a little more water if necessary until both are half tender. Add spinach and Garam Masala and simmer a further 10 minutes. Serve with rice or chapatis.

PROTEIN-RICH DISHES

Protein sources in vegetarian meals come from cheese, milk, eggs, yoghurt, lentils and soy bean products.

Fresh bean curd comes in various forms—soft, firm, fried. Look in the refrigerator section of Asian shops or health food stores. Fermented soy bean cakes (tempeh) are sold frozen. Dried bean curd (in sheets or sticks) is in packets and has a long shelf life. Red (pickled) bean curd, in jars, is the Asian equivalent of gorgonzola. It keeps well and a small amount adds a lot of zip to a dish.

Fresh cheese for Indian dishes is quick and easy to make (see Fresh Cheese Koftas in Creamy Sauce on p. 72). Even quicker is to buy baked ricotta. It is suited to recipes where cheese is cut in cubes but not a recipe in which the cheese has to be moulded.

Lentils and dried peas or beans make delicious soups, purées, curries, rissoles, salads or braised dishes.

It is important to buy firm bean curd, as soft bean curd will disintegrate with this style of cooking. If all you can get is soft bean curd, make the sauce and pour it over but don't try to fry the bean curd or simmer it for long.

BRAISED BEAN CURD, SZECHWAN STYLE
Serves 4

- 500 g (1 lb) block firm bean curd
- ¼ cup peanut oil
- 1 tablespoon finely chopped garlic
- 3 teaspoons finely chopped fresh ginger
- 3 tablespoons hoi sin sauce
- 3 tablespoons bean sauce (min sze jeung)
- ½–1 teaspoon chilli bean sauce
- 1 teaspoon oriental sesame oil
- 1 teaspoon sugar
- 1 small red capsicum

After removing bean curd from plastic pouch, wrap in paper towels and press gently to remove excess moisture. The kind I buy is 10 cm (4 inches) square and 5 cm (2 inches) deep. Cut block into 32 x 2.5 cm (1 inch) cubes.

Reserve 1 tablespoon of peanut oil and heat remainder in a wok. Fry half the bean curd at a time until cubes are pale golden, drain on paper towels. Pour off remaining oil and clean wok with paper towels.

Heat reserved oil and on low heat fry garlic and ginger, stirring, until pale gold, about 2 minutes. If they start to brown remove from heat immediately and pour in rest of ingredients mixed with ½ cup water. Add bean curd and simmer, covered, for 10 minutes. Cut red capsicum into bite-size squares and toss through bean curd for 1 minute, not long enough to diminish its crisp texture. Serve immediately with rice.

Note   I have also cooked this dish without deep-frying the bean curd. While the bean curd is not as deeply golden, it is softer in texture.

SPINACH AND CHEESE
Serves 4

- *2 bunches English spinach*
- *250 g (8 oz) baked ricotta*
- *1 tablespoon ghee or butter*
- *1 teaspoon Panch Phora (see p. 1)*
- *1 teaspoon turmeric*
- *1 teaspoon ground cummin*
- *1 teaspoon finely grated fresh ginger*
- *1 cup natural yoghurt*
- *salt to taste*
- *1 teaspoon Garam Masala (see p. 2)*

Wash spinach in several changes of cold water and put leaves into a stainless steel pan with just moisture that clings to leaves. Cover and steam for 10 to 12 minutes or until tender. Drain and chop. Cut baked ricotta or home-made cheese (see p. 72) into cubes.

Heat ghee and fry Panch Phora until mustard seeds pop. Add turmeric, cummin and ginger and stir for a minute, then add spinach and mix well. Stir in yoghurt, season with salt, and when mixture is heated through add cheese and simmer gently for 10 minutes. Sprinkle with Garam Masala towards end of cooking. Serve with rice or flat bread.

If your meat-eating friends try this recipe, they will find it hard to believe it is vegetarian.

SAVOURY TEMPEH MINCE
Serves 6

- *250 g (8 oz) tempeh*
- *½ cup peanut oil*
- *2 large onions, finely chopped*
- *4 cloves garlic, finely chopped*
- *2 teaspoons finely chopped fresh ginger*
- *2 or 3 fresh chillies, sliced or pickled hot chillies*
- *1 tablespoon soy sauce*
- *½ teaspoon ground black pepper*
- *500 g (1 lb) potatoes*
- *salt to taste*

Let tempeh thaw at room temperature, then cut blocks into thin slices before cutting across into tiny dice. Reserve a tablespoon of oil and heat remainder in a wok or small deep pan and when very hot fry half the tempeh at a time until golden brown. Lift out on perforated spoon and drain on paper towels. Pour off any remaining oil and heat wok with reserved oil. Fry onions, garlic, ginger and chillies over gentle heat, stirring frequently, until onions are translucent and start to brown. Add tempeh, soy sauce and pepper, turn off heat.

Peel and finely dice potatoes, drop into lightly salted boiling water, boil until soft, drain in colander. Mix into tempeh mixture, mashing potatoes slightly, and add salt to taste. Serve with rice.

Note Mixture may also be shaped into patties and shallow-fried, first dipping into beaten egg and breadcrumbs. Accompany with a salad of sliced tomato and cucumber.

There must be as many variations on this ubiquitous recipe as there are cooks! Here is a quickly made version using the small red lentils found in every supermarket. This is the great Indian staple, dhal.

Lentil Purée
Serves 6

- *1 cup red lentils*
- *2 tablespoons ghee or oil*
- *1 onion, finely sliced*
- *2 cloves garlic, finely chopped*
- *1 teaspoon finely chopped fresh ginger*
- *½ teaspoon turmeric*
- *salt to taste*
- *1 teaspoon Garam Masala (see p. 2)*

Pick over lentils and discard any small stones. Wash well, removing those that float. Drain in a sieve for 10 minutes.

Heat ghee or oil in a saucepan and fry onion, garlic and ginger until onion is brown. Add turmeric and stir once or twice, add drained lentils and fry for a couple of minutes. Add 2½ cups hot water and bring to the boil. Turn heat down, cover pan and simmer for 20 minutes. Add salt and Garam Masala and cook until lentils are very soft. If too much liquid remains, uncover to help evaporation. Garnish with fried onions—they must be deep golden brown—and serve with rice or flat bread.

One of my favourite dishes, fresh cheese and peas in a spicy tomato gravy. In India they would make cheese at home, but you may substitute baked ricotta.

Peas and Fresh Cheese
Serves 4 to 6

- *500 g (1 lb) baked ricotta, diced or home-made cheese (see recipe for Fresh Cheese Koftas, p. 72)*
  - *2 tablespoons oil or ghee*
  - *1 cup finely chopped onion*
  - *2 teaspoons finely chopped garlic*
- *2 teaspoons finely chopped fresh ginger*
  - *1 tablespoon ground coriander*
  - *2 teaspoons ground cummin*
  - *1 teaspoon ground turmeric*
  - *½ teaspoon chilli powder*
- *3 ripe tomatoes peeled, seeded and chopped*
  - *500 g (1 lb) fresh or frozen peas*
  - *1 teaspoon salt or to taste*
- *1½ teaspoons Garam Masala (see p. 2)*
- *¼ cup chopped fresh mint or coriander*

Heat oil or ghee in a heavy saucepan and fry onion, garlic and ginger over medium low heat, stirring occasionally, until translucent and starting to turn golden. Sprinkle in coriander, cummin, turmeric and chilli and stir for 2 minutes or until spices smell fragrant and darken slightly.

Add tomatoes, fresh peas, salt and Garam Masala, cover and simmer until tomatoes are pulpy and peas are cooked. If using frozen peas don't add until tomatoes are soft. Add cheese and simmer for 10 minutes, then sprinkle with mint or coriander and serve with rice or Indian bread.

TOFU KEBABS, BARBECUED
Serves 4

- *375 g (12 oz) firm bean curd*
- *1 teaspoon crushed garlic*
- *½ teaspoon salt*
- *1 teaspoon finely grated fresh ginger*
- *good grinding of black pepper*
- *½ teaspoon turmeric*
- *1 teaspoon ground cummin*
- *½ teaspoon dried oregano*
- *2 tablespoons soy sauce*
- *1 tablespoon oriental sesame oil*
- *1 tablespoon lemon juice*

Cut bean curd into 2 cm (¾ inch) cubes. Combine all remaining ingredients in a bowl and add to cubes, turning them to ensure all surfaces are covered with marinade. Cover and leave for 30 minutes. Soak bamboo skewers in water while tofu is marinating to prevent them burning.

Cook tofu over barbecue or under a preheated griller for about 2 minutes each side until browned. Serve with rice or chapatis and accompanied by a bowl of finely sliced cucumbers in yoghurt.

A perfect dish for those preferring hot flavours. It may be toned down by reducing the amount of chilli bean sauce.

BEAN CURD WITH HOT BEAN SAUCE
Serves 6

- 500 g (1 lb) firm bean curd
- 2 tablespoons peanut oil
- ¼ cup finely chopped spring onion
- 2 teaspoons finely chopped garlic
- 2 teaspoons finely chopped fresh ginger
- 1 tablespoon ground bean sauce (mor sze jeung)
- ½–1 teaspoon chilli bean paste
- ¼ cup tomato ketchup
- 1 tablespoon light soy sauce
- 2 teaspoons red bean curd, mashed (see Note)
- 2 teaspoons cornflour
- 1 teaspoon oriental sesame oil

Dice the bean curd into 2 cm (¾ inch) cubes and drop into a pan of boiling water. Boil for 3 to 4 minutes until bean curd is heated through, then drain in a colander.

Heat peanut oil and fry spring onion for a few seconds, stirring before adding garlic and ginger. Continue to fry over low heat until fragrant and starting to turn golden. Add various sauces and mashed red bean curd mixed with ⅔ cup stock or water. Stir until boiling, then stir in cornflour mixed smoothly with a tablespoon of water until mixture thickens.

Add diced bean curd and gently turn in the sauce until coated. Sprinkle sesame oil over and mix. Serve on steamed rice.

Note Red bean curd is the Chinese equivalent of gorgonzola cheese—it is fermented and packed in jars or cans with chilli which gives it the red colour. Used in small quantities, but keeps well even after the jar is opened.

SAVOURY KIDNEY BEANS
Serves 6

- *250 g (8 oz) red or brown kidney beans*
  - *1 onion stuck with 4 cloves*
    - *3 cardamom pods*
    - *1 teaspoon salt*
    - *2 tablespoons oil*
  - *1 tablespoon ghee, optional*
    - *2 onions, finely chopped*
  - *3 cloves garlic, finely chopped*
- *2 teaspoons finely chopped fresh ginger*
  - *2 teaspoons ground cummin*
    - *1 teaspoon turmeric*
- *1 cup chopped ripe tomatoes or canned tomatoes*
  - *½ teaspoon Garam Masala (see p. 2)*
    - *¼ cup chopped fresh coriander*

Soak beans in plenty of water overnight. Rinse, put into a saucepan with fresh water to cover onion and cardamom pods. Bring to the boil, lower heat and simmer, covered, for 1 hour, then add salt and continue cooking until beans are very tender.

In another pan heat oil and ghee and cook chopped onions, garlic and ginger over low heat, stirring occasionally, until onions are very soft, translucent and starting to turn golden—about 20 minutes. Add cummin and turmeric and fry, stirring, for a few seconds, then add tomatoes and beans together with about a cup of their cooking liquid. Cover and simmer for 20 minutes, then sprinkle with Garam Masala and coriander and cook 5 minutes. Serve with rice or chapatis.

Savoury Chick Peas
Serves 6

- *250 g (8 oz) dried chick peas*
- *1 teaspoon salt or to taste*
- *2 tablespoons oil or ghee*
- *sprig of fresh curry leaves*
- *1 teaspoon Panch Phora (see p. 1)*
- *1 large onion, finely chopped*
- *1 tablespoon finely chopped fresh ginger*
- *1 teaspoon turmeric*
- *¼ teaspoon asafoetida, optional*
- *3 ripe tomatoes, peeled and chopped*
- *1 tablespoon lemon juice*
- *1 teaspoon Garam Masala (see p. 2)*
- *¼ cup chopped coriander or mint leaves*

Pick over the chick peas and discard any discoloured ones. Soak in plenty of cold water overnight. Drain, cover with fresh water and cook until tender. Add salt only after peas have softened. This will take about 1½ hours unless a pressure cooker is used. The peas should be very soft but not falling apart. Drain, reserving cooking liquid.

Heat oil or ghee in a saucepan and fry curry leaves and Panch Phora until they spatter and pop. Add onion and ginger and cook on medium low heat until onion is translucent and turning deep golden. Add turmeric, salt to taste, asafoetida and fry for a minute, then add tomatoes. Cover and cook until tomatoes are pulpy. Add chick peas and enough of reserved cooking liquid to cover base of pan. Simmer until gravy is reduced and thick, sprinkle with lemon juice, Garam Masala and chopped herb and serve with rice or flat bread.

Only home-made cheese (panir) is suitable for this recipe—cottage and ricotta cheese don't work.

Fresh Cheese Koftas in Creamy Sauce
Serves 4

- 2 litres (8 cups) full cream milk
- ¼ cup lemon juice
- ¼ cup finely chopped coriander leaves
- 2 tablespoons chopped sultanas
- 2 tablespoons chopped almonds
- 2 teaspoons chopped fresh chillies, optional
- salt and pepper to taste
- oil and ghee for deep-frying

Sauce
- 1 tablespoon ghee or butter
- 2 teaspoons finely chopped garlic
- 1 onion, finely chopped
- 3 tablespoons tomato paste
- 1½ teaspoons salt
- 1 tablespoon sugar
- 1 tablespoon fine shreds of ginger
- ½ cup cream
- 1 teaspoon Garam Masala (see p. 2)
- ¼ cup chopped fresh coriander

Bring milk to the boil, stir in lemon juice, remove from heat and let stand for 15 minutes, then drain in muslin-lined colander. (Save the whey, you will be using it in the sauce.) Leave for 30 minutes. When as much moisture as possible has been removed, break curds into pieces and knead vigorously until smooth and palm of hand feels greasy. Divide into 8 equal portions and roll each into a ball.

Combine coriander, sultanas, almonds and chillies, adding salt and pepper to taste. Make a depression in each ball and fill with some of coriander mixture, then mould ball around filling again, making a smooth surface without cracks. Heat about 2 cups oil with ¼ cup ghee to flavour it and fry cheese koftas on medium heat until golden brown all over, then drain on paper towels.

SAUCE In a heavy pan melt ghee or butter and cook garlic and onion until soft and translucent. Add tomato paste, salt, sugar and ginger and stir into 1½ cups whey. Cover and simmer for 10 minutes. Stir in cream. Simmer koftas in sauce for 10 minutes. Sprinkle with Garam Masala and coriander and serve with Indian bread or rice.

RICE, NOODLES AND BREADS

Grains—mostly rice and wheat—are the staple foods of Asia. Every spiced dish is served with rice or, in India, chapatis (unleavened bread). For best results, choose the right kind of rice for the food of various countries. For an Indian meal try basmati or dehra dun rice—long, slender grains with a fragrance all their own. For Thai meals, use jasmine rice; for Chinese or Japanese meals use short or medium grain rice, though long grain rice is gaining popularity. Avoid converted rice or instant rice. The texture, flavour and mouth feel is not correct in Asian meals.

For perfectly cooked rice, measure rice in cups, wash and drain well, put into a heavy based saucepan. For each 1 cup of rice, add 1½ cups water. Add salt if desired. Bring to a boil, cover tightly, turn heat very low and cook for 20 minutes.

Sweet and Spicy Pilau

Serves 6 to 8

- *500 g (1 lb) basmati or dehra dun rice*
- *½ teaspoon saffron strands*
- *2 tablespoons ghee*
- *5 cardamom pods, bruised*
- *5 whole cloves*
- *5 cm (2 inch) stick cinnamon*
- *1½ teaspoons salt or to taste*
- *finely grated rind of 1 orange or lemon*
- *½ cup orange juice or ¼ cup lemon juice*
- *2 tablespoons sugar*

Wash rice, changing water several times. Drain in a colander for at least 30 minutes. Roast saffron strands in a dry pan over low heat for a minute or until colour darkens slightly—but do not let them scorch. Turn onto a saucer and when cool and brittle, crush to powder with back of a spoon. Dissolve in 2 tablespoons boiling water.

Heat ghee in heavy saucepan and fry whole spices and rice, stirring with a metal spoon, for about 3 minutes. Add 4 cups hot water, saffron, salt, citrus rind and juice, and sugar. Stir well as it comes to the boil, then turn heat low, cover tightly and cook for 20 minutes without lifting lid. Uncover, let steam escape and remove whole spices. Fluff rice with fork and serve with Fresh Cheese Koftas in Creamy Sauce (see p. 72).

Rice in Coconut Milk with Fried Cashews
Serves 6

- *500 g (1 lb) basmati or other long grain rice*
- *2 tablespoons ghee or oil*
- *2 medium onions, finely sliced*
- *2 sprigs fresh curry leaves*
- *½ teaspoon whole black peppercorns*
- *5 cm (2 inch) stick cinnamon*
- *5 cardamom pods, bruised*
- *5 whole cloves*
- *1 scant teaspoon ground turmeric*
- *1 x 400 mL can coconut milk*
- *2 teaspoons salt or to taste*
- *oil for deep-frying*
- *100 g (3½ oz) raw cashews*

Wash rice well and drain in a colander for at least 30 minutes. Heat ghee in a heavy saucepan and fry onions, curry leaves and whole spices. Stir frequently. Add turmeric and rice, stir and fry until rice is coated with ghee, about 3 minutes.

Mix coconut milk with water to make 4 cups. Add to pan, stir in salt and bring to the boil. Cover pan tightly, turn heat very low and cook for 20 to 25 minutes until coconut milk is absorbed.

Heat peanut oil and fry cashews, stirring constantly so they colour evenly. Serve rice hot, garnished with fried cashews.

In India this is served as a snack or at breakfast, but may also be served as a main meal.

SEMOLINA AND VEGETABLE PILAU
Serves 4 to 6

- *1½ tablespoons ghee*
- *2 cups semolina*
- *3 tablespoons oil*
- *1 teaspoon black mustard seeds*
- *2 sprigs fresh curry leaves*
- *1 tablespoon urad dhal or mung dhal*
- *1 tablespoon channa dhal*
- *3 dried red chillies, snipped into pieces*
- *2 large onions, finely chopped*
- *2 fresh chillies, sliced*
- *2 teaspoons finely chopped fresh ginger*
- *½ cup diced capsicum*
- *½ cup thawed frozen peas*
- *½ cup tiny broccoli florets*
- *1½ teaspoons salt*
- *2 teaspoons ghee*
- *lemon wedges*

Use a heavy saucepan with well fitting lid and heat ghee until melted. Fry semolina, stirring constantly, until golden, then turn into a bowl and wipe out pan with paper towels.

Heat oil in pan and fry mustard seeds, curry leaves, dhals and dried chillies. Discard chilli seeds if preferred. As soon as dhal turns golden add onions and fry, stirring, until onions start to colour. Add fresh chillies, ginger and vegetables, stirring for about 8 minutes. Add 2 cups hot water, stir in salt and when it boils add semolina and stir constantly until it becomes quite dry. Cover pan with well fitting lid and leave on very low heat until semolina is tender, 5 to 10 minutes. Add ghee and fork it through. Serve in small bowls with wedges of lemon for squeezing over each portion. If using this as a main dish, accompany it with a bowl of natural yoghurt for nutritional balance.

Rice with Red Lentils

Serves 6

- *1½ cups basmati rice*
- *1½ cups red lentils*
- *3 tablespoons ghee*
- *2 onions, finely sliced*
- *4 cardamom pods, bruised*
- *5 cm (2 inch) stick of cinnamon*
- *1 teaspoon Garam Masala (see p. 2)*
- *2 teaspoons salt or to taste*

Wash rice thoroughly several times in cold water. Drain in a colander for at least 30 minutes. Wash lentils well removing any that look less than perfect. Drain.

Heat ghee in a heavy based saucepan with a well fitting lid and fry onion over low heat until golden brown. Remove half and reserve for garnishing. Add spices, rice and lentils to pan and fry, stirring constantly, for 3 minutes. Add 4 cups hot water, salt and Garam Masala and stir while bringing to the boil. Cover tightly, turn heat very low and simmer for 20 minutes without lifting lid. Take a look and if all liquid is absorbed it is ready. If not, replace lid and cook a further 5 minutes. Serve garnished with reserved onions.

CHAPATIS
Makes 20 to 24

- *3 cups atta or roti flour*
- *1 teaspoon salt*
- *1 tablespoon ghee or oil*
- *1 cup water*

Put flour into mixing bowl with salt and rub in ghee or oil. Make a well in centre and pour in water. Mix to a firm but not stiff dough. Add more water or flour as needed. Knead dough for at least 10 minutes until smooth and elastic and form into a ball. Place back into bowl, cover with plastic wrap and stand for at least 1 hour.

Form dough into 20 to 24 walnut-size balls and keep covered. Roll out on lightly floured surface into thin circles and lay them ready to cook, not touching as they will stick. Heat a heavy frying pan or griddle and cook chapatis, individually, starting with those which were rolled first. Cook for 1 minute on first side, turn over with frying spatula. When cooking second side, help chapati rise by pressing around edges with spatula or folded tea towel. This makes the bread puff. Wrap in a clean tea towel to keep warm until all chapatis are cooked.

PURIS

Follow instructions for chapatis to stage where they are rolled into thin circles. Heat about 2.5 cm (1 inch) oil in a deep frying pan and fry puris, one at a time, spooning hot oil over until they puff and swell, and are golden brown all over. Drain on paper towels. Serve immediately with Indian curries.

As you will see by reading the recipe, parathas are not the sort of thing you can toss off in 5 minutes—but they are delicious and well worth the time taken. The good thing about them is that they can be cooked, cooled, wrapped tightly in foil and frozen. Then, when required, they can be heated in a moderate oven, still wrapped in foil.

Parathas
Makes 10

- *1½ cups atta flour*
- *1½ cups plain white flour or roti flour*
- *1½ teaspoons salt*
- *6–8 tablespoons ghee*
- *1¼ cups water*
- *extra ghee for cooking*

Sift flours and salt into a mixing bowl. Add 1 tablespoon of ghee, rubbing it in with fingertips as if making pastry. Add 1¼ cups water and mix to a firm dough. Knead for at least 10 minutes until dough is elastic. Form into a ball, return to mixing bowl, cover with plastic wrap and set aside for 1 hour.

Divide dough into 10 portions and roll each into a ball. Melt remaining ghee and leave to cool slightly. Roll dough into paper-thin circles on a lightly floured board. Place 2 teaspoons melted ghee in the centre of each circle and spread over the entire circle with your hand. Using a sharp knife make a cut from centre of each circle to edge. Starting at cut, roll each circle into a tight cone. Press apex and base of cone together and flatten gently.

Lightly flour the board again and roll out dough into circles. Do this carefully and don't press too hard. The circles should be slightly thicker than originally.

Grease a heavy frying pan or griddle with extra ghee and cook parathas until they are golden on both sides. Add more ghee to pan as required. Keep covered with a clean tea towel until all parathas are cooked. Serve warm or at room temperature.

Rotis with Vegetable Filling
Makes 10

- *1 quantity Chapati dough (see p. 79)*
  - *1 cup finely grated cauliflower*
- *1 teaspoon finely grated fresh ginger*
  - *½ teaspoon salt or to taste*
- *1 teaspoon Garam Masala (see p. 2)*
  - *pinch of chilli powder, optional*
    - *squeeze of lemon juice*
    - *3 tablespoons ghee or oil*

Make chapati dough, knead hard, cover and leave to rest as described on page 79. Divide dough into 20 pieces of equal size and roll each into a smooth ball. On a lightly floured surface roll out thinly to the size of a saucer. Combine remaining ingredients except ghee or oil. Fill and seal as described on page 82 for Savoury Stuffed Rotis. Cook in the same way until golden brown both sides. Serve warm or at room temperature as soon as possible after cooking and accompany with a bowl of thick yoghurt, either plain or flavoured with a couple of spoonfuls of Fresh Mint Chutney (see p. 40).

You don't have to make a quantity of filling specially for these filled breads—leftovers mashed smoothly are very suitable.

SAVOURY STUFFED ROTIS
Makes 12

- Lentil Purée (see p. 66), Dry Potato Curry (see p. 47),
   Spicy Mashed Potatoes (see p. 46)
   or Sweet-sour Potatoes (see p. 45)
- 1 quantity chapati dough (see p. 79)
- 3 tablespoons ghee or oil

If using Lentil Purée, cook it so it is dry enough to mound in the spoon. Mash any pieces of potato so they can be spread flat. After chapati dough has rested, divide it into 16 equal portions, roll into balls and keep covered.

On a lightly floured surface roll out each very thinly to the size of a saucer and as perfectly round as possible. Leaving a rim of 1 cm (½ inch) around edge, spread a tablespoon of filling in centre. Dampen edge and place another saucer-size circle of dough on top, pressing firmly to seal. Continue making rotis with remaining mixture but keep them separate with squares of greaseproof paper because they stick if allowed to touch.

When all are made, heat a heavy frying pan and melt a teaspoon of ghee. Place one roti in the pan and cook on medium heat, spreading another teaspoon of ghee on top side. Turn roti after 1 minute and continue to cook and turn, pressing edges gently so they come in contact with pan, until golden brown both sides. Stack in a deep basket lined with a tea towel and cover to keep warm. Serve as soon as possible, with a bowl of yoghurt dip.

THAI-STYLE RICE NOODLES
Serves 4

- *8 dried shiitake (Chinese) mushrooms*
- *375 g (12 oz) fine rice vermicelli*
- *15 g (½ oz) dried wood fungus*
- *250 g (8 oz) tender asparagus*
- *125 g (4 oz) firm bean curd*
- *3 tablespoons peanut oil*
- *2 teaspoons finely chopped garlic*
- *1 teaspoon finely chopped fresh ginger*
- *3 teaspoons green peppercorns in brine, crushed*
- *1 cup finely sliced green beans*
- *½ cup julienned carrot*
- *3 tablespoons Maggi Seasoning (see Note p. 9)*
- *3 teaspoons sugar*

Soak mushrooms in very hot water for at least 30 minutes, then squeeze out excess moisture and cut caps in thin slices. Put rice vermicelli in a bowl and pour boiling water over. Soak for 3 minutes or until tender, then drain. Soak wood fungus in cold water for 10 minutes, then cut into bite-size pieces. Cut asparagus into short lengths, discarding any tough base of stem. Slice bean curd and cut slices into bite-size squares.

Heat oil in a wok and fry garlic and ginger over gentle heat, stirring, until fragrant. Add bean curd and stir-fry for 2 minutes. Add peppercorns, mushrooms, beans, carrot, asparagus and wood fungus. Stir-fry for 2 minutes. Mix Maggi Seasoning with sugar and 3 tablespoons water, pour into wok, cover and simmer for 2 minutes. Add rice vermicelli, toss and stir until heated through. Taste, adjust seasoning if necessary and serve hot.

BEAN THREAD VERMICELLI WITH TEMPEH
Serves 6

- *150 g (5 oz) bean thread vermicelli*
- *12 dried shiitake (Chinese) mushrooms*
- *3 tablespoons peanut oil*
- *2 teaspoons finely chopped fresh ginger*
- *½ cup finely sliced spring onions*
- *1 teaspoon chilli bean sauce*
- *3 tablespoons light soy sauce*
- *1 quantity Savoury Tempeh Mince (see p. 65—omit potatoes)*
- *chilli flower and coriander leaves to garnish*

Cook bean thread vermicelli in boiling water for 10 minutes or until soft. Drain in a colander and cut very long strands into shorter lengths for easier handling. Soak mushrooms in very hot water for 30 minutes, squeeze out excess water and chop mushroom caps, discarding stems. Reserve water.

Heat wok, add peanut oil and when hot stir-fry mushrooms, ginger and spring onions for about 3 minutes. Add sauces mixed with ½ cup mushroom soaking water, cover and simmer for 5 minutes or until mushrooms are softened. Add prepared savoury tempeh and bean thread vermicelli and toss until well mixed and heated through. Serve garnished with chilli flower and sprigs of coriander leaves.

GLOSSARY

You can find most of these ingredients in Asian stores and many are sold in supermarkets, etc.

ATTA FLOUR Fine wholemeal flour (or an 80/20 mixture of wholemeal and white) for making chapatis and other flat breads. I prefer roti flour or sharps (a grade to which flour is milled, leaving it slightly granular). It makes softer chapatis. Both are sold at Indian shops or some health food stores. Substitute fine wholemeal mixed with plain white flour.

BAMBOO SHOOTS Sold in cans. Winter bamboo shoots are more tender.

BEAN CURD Made from soy beans and high in protein. It is available fresh in various forms—soft, firm or fried. Soft bean curd has the consistency of junket. Firm bean curd (pressed bean curd) is sold in 400 g or 500 g (1 lb) blocks. It's easier to cook because it does not break up when stirred. Fried bean curd comes in golden brown cubes, creamy white and spongy inside. All types may be found in the refrigerator section of Asian stores. Fresh bean curd may be kept refrigerated for up to 3 days.

BEAN SAUCE There are two kinds of bean sauce: one is smooth, labelled 'refined bean sauce'; the other has pieces of soy bean in it.

BEAN THREAD VERMICELLI Transparent noodles made from the starch of mung beans. Purchase in packets divided into 50 g or 60 g skeins.

CARDAMOM There are two varieties—large, brownish-black pods and small green ones. The small variety is preferable. It should be fragrant and well packed in airtight containers if purchased ground. No substitute.

CHILLIES Fresh chillies range from large, sweet, mild capsicums which are used as a vegetable, to small, fiery hot varieties which should be handled with care as the volatile oils can cause much discomfort. Wear gloves when chopping, slicing or removing seeds. Chopped chillies in jars may be substituted, and also Sambal ulek (oelek) which is a mixture of fresh chillies and salt, or Tabasco Pepper Sauce (use 1 teaspoon for each hot chilli).

CHILLI BEAN SAUCE This is super hot, a mixture of salted soy beans and chillies in oil. Use sparingly.

CINNAMON True cinnamon is pale brown and is usually rolled into quills with 4 or 5 layers of fine bark one within the other.

CLOVES The dried flower buds of a tree native to South East Asia. Use sparingly. Nearest substitute is allspice.

COCONUT MILK Buy unsweetened coconut milk in cans. If it's very thick, dilute with 2 parts water to 1 of coconut milk. If it pours readily like cream, use it diluted with an equal amount of water. Unused coconut milk should be frozen immediately in ice cube trays as it does not keep well, even in the refrigerator.

CORIANDER The dried seeds, ground finely, are used in almost every curry. Sometimes they are roasted first to subtly emphasise the flavour. The fresh herb is also used, and in Thailand the root is an important flavour in curry pastes. The leaves are used for garnishing and as an extra flavour.

CUMMIN Purchased either as whole seeds or ground, this spice has a lemony fragrance and is a major component of curries.

CURRY LEAVES Small leaflets making up a compound leaf, these give great flavour to many dishes. They are increasingly becoming available fresh. Some nurseries and Asian stores now sell young plants which grow in a temperate climate if sheltered from frosts.

FENNEL SEEDS Larger and lighter coloured than cummin, they have a licorice flavour and are used only in certain dishes.

Fenugreek seeds One of the essential ingredients in curry powder, these pale beige seeds do have a bitter undertone and are used in small quantities.

Galangal Two species of galangal, greater and lesser, are used in Asian food. Greater galangal is used throughout South East Asia. Outside Asia it is available in jars, its slices large and white. It may also be purchased frozen, dried or powdered, the latter being known as laos powder.

Ghee Clarified butter, or pure butter fat. Essential in Indian cooking, it can be heated to high temperatures without burning. Made in Australia.

Ginger Fresh rhizomes are usually available at any greengrocer. Dried ground ginger is no substitute in Asian cooking.

Green peppercorns Sometimes available fresh, but most readily found bottled or canned in brine.

Hoi sin sauce A thick, dark, sweet bean sauce.

Kaffir lime leaves Used in Thai cooking. Sold fresh, frozen or dried.

Kalonji seeds (nigella) Small black seeds with a little point on one end. Lovely nutty flavour. No substitute.

Lemon grass Grows easily in tropical and temperate climates. The pale green or white portion at the base of the stem imparts a lemony fragrance. Substitute 2 strips of thinly peeled lemon rind.

Lily buds Also known as 'golden needles', these are the dried buds of a variety of day lily and may be omitted without ruining the dish.

Maggi seasoning A Swiss sauce similar to Golden Mountain Sauce which is used widely in Asia. Maggi has added monosodium glutamate.

Okra A furry green pod very popular in India. Buy only tender ones. If mature they are impossibly stringy.

Palm sugar Obtained from various tropical palms, it has a distinct flavour but may be substituted by brown sugar.

Pandan leaf Sold fresh, frozen or dried, this broad green leaf of *Pandanus latifolia* imparts a delicate flavour.

Rice For Indian cooking, use basmati or Dehra Dun rice, both very similar with fine, long grains which cook up very fluffy and separate. In Thailand and other South East Asian countries jasmine rice is preferred.

Roti flour *See* **Atta flour**.

Sambal ulek (oelek) *See* **Chillies**.

Sesame oil When sesame oil is called for in Eastern recipes, it is oriental sesame oil made from toasted sesame seeds.

Tamarind Fruit of a tropical tree, tamarind imparts acidity to many dishes. It is sold dried, puréed or instant. The dried pulp has the truest flavour. Soak in hot water, dissolve pulp, strain. You can also dissolve the puréed or instant tamarind in hot water, but some of these are too acidic or salty. Check strength before adding, adjust quantity accordingly.

Tempeh Fermented compressed soy bean cakes sold either natural or flavoured. Found in the freezer section of Asian or health food stores.

Turmeric A rhizome of the ginger family, this one has bright yellow flesh under its brown skin. Mostly available dried and ground.

Water chestnuts Available in cans. After opening, store in water in refrigerator for a week, changing water daily.

Wood fungus, dried Also known as 'cloud ear fungus' or 'wood ears'. After soaking for 10 minutes it swells and turns into translucent brown cloud shapes. A flavourless ingredient, used for its texture.

Yam bean Known as jicama (pronounce 'j' as 'h') in Mexico, the various Asian names for this delicious, crisp white tuber are bang kwang (in Singapore/Malaysia) and saagott (in China).

Yoghurt The best yoghurt to use is natural yoghurt, not the skim milk variety which seems to have a greater acidity and overpowers other flavours.

Index